A HANDBOOK FOR

Writing Formal Papers

FROM CONCEPT TO CONCLUSION

Fourth Edition

NORMAN W. STEINAKER • TERRY A. BUSTILLOS

NATIONAL UNIVERSITY

Custom Publishing

New York   Boston   San Francisco
London   Toronto   Sydney   Tokyo   Singapore   Madrid
Mexico City   Munich   Paris   Cape Town   Hong Kong   Montreal

**Pearson
Custom Publishing**
is a division of

PEARSON

www.pearsonhighered.com

ISBN 10: 0-536-64742-9
ISBN 13: 978-0-536-64742-9

Table of Contents

In the formal writing process you need to be organized, thoughtful, and clear. Formal writing is a pristine exercise in clarity, continuity, and cogent thinking. There are five words or steps which can illuminate this writing process. They are define, describe, detail, discuss, and determine. These steps are intrinsic to the process of writing and to the organization, clarity, and thoughtfulness of your paper. They are the sequential steps that writers of formal papers follow. In the formal writing process these five sequential steps are the key to writing a successful paper that brings understanding and meaning to the reader. You need to be continually cognizant of them as you write your paper. Remember also that formal writing, while it has a style and character of its own as well as a particular format, should also be lively and interesting to the reader. The careful sequencing of these five steps in the development of your paper, done with craft and skill, can infuse liveliness and interest into your work. Again, the five words are define, describe, detail, discuss, and determine.

Define

The first obligation you have to the reader is to define the topic of your paper. Definition consists of a clear, concise, and coherent characterization of the topic being studied. This should be done in the first few paragraphs of your paper, preferably in the first paragraph. Let the reader know immediately the subject and focus of the paper, so there is a clear understanding of the purpose and what is to come in the paper. In defining the paper you should indicate the limits and parameters of the paper. It is essential that this be done early in the paper so the reader can quickly and clearly comprehend the topic as well as its focus and limitations. If you are writing a research proposal or research study you need to define the questions or issues you are addressing and how you have approached them. Through the clear and careful exposition of the topic and issues in your paper, the reader can make a decision as to how the content could be used for personal or professional purposes. Definition is the equivalent of memory and translation in the cognitive taxonomy and exposure in the experiential taxonomy (Steinaker & Bell, 1979).

Describe

After the definition is clearly, concisely, and coherently stated, you will need to describe the topic so the reader understands the focus of your paper. You will need to provide, in the introduction or first section of your paper, some additional information to make it clear to the reader how you have limited and focused the topic of your paper. You will also need to establish the importance of the paper in the field. To do this you should provide the reader with a few salient citations and specifics about the topic. The reader should not only know what the topic is, but should have a clear understanding of why it is important. The reader should know, through the specific information you have provided, the importance of the topic and how it is to be focused and developed. You should also inform the reader why you have selected this topic. All of these elements describe your paper and give it substance, meaning, and purpose. When you have completed both the definition and the description, you have completed the introduction or first section of your paper. This describing process corresponds to translation and interpretation in the cognitive taxonomy and to participation in the experiential taxonomy.

Detail

In the review of literature and method sections of the paper you detail or tell about what researchers, writers, and commentators have reported about the topic you have selected and how you have organized your study. It is your task to detail and inform for the reader, as objectively as possible, the information you have found through your reading and reviewing the literature. You simply relate the information without personal comment and without interpretation. You note, cite, and tell what has been done in the field and what you have discovered through your own review of literature. Nothing more is needed and nothing more should be done. You will need to organize your detailed information into categories and subcategories in the review of literature to clarify it, to explicate it, and to structure your paper for the reader. This kind of organization is always very helpful to the reader. You need to remember the review of literature provides the evidentiary basis for your discussion. When doing a research paper you will include a method section in which you detail the organization, the structure, and the process developed for your study. You will include information on data collection and analyses of these data. You must also include a results section in which you report your findings. These further add to your evidentiary base for your conclusions and your recommendations. You may utilize existing research models or you may develop a model specific to your study. The detail step in writing corresponds to the application and analysis levels of the cognitive taxonomy and the identification level of the experiential taxonomy.

Discuss

This step in the formal writing process is done, and logically so, in the discussion section of your paper. If you are doing a review of literature only, this will be the final section of your paper. If you are doing a qualitative or quantitative study, this section will follow the method and results sections and will be the concluding section of your study. In a research study you will discuss not only the review of literature, but also your method and findings from the study. For review of literature papers you first summarize what you have found in the literature you reviewed. Then you interpret the literature usually, but not necessarily, by category. The elements you need to consider are as follows: You note consistencies and inconsistencies and you bridge the gaps. You compare and contrast. You construct and deconstruct. You identify the important and eliminate the non pertinent. You build your own perspective through this process. You let the reader know that you have understood, applied, and analyzed the information and the findings thoroughly and completely. Your discussion must be straight forward and professional. It must reflect the careful consideration you have given to the topic and the thoroughness of your review of literature. If you are doing an qualitative or quantitative study, this section follows the method and results section. You not only review the literature, but you incorporate the review with your method and your findings and bring them together in the discussion section of your study. This process in your paper corresponds to the analysis and synthesis levels of the cognitive taxonomy and to the internalization level of the experiential taxonomy.

Determine

In the final section of your paper you make determinations about the topic and what you have learned. Here you draw conclusions and make recommendations. These conclusions and recommendations should be consistent within the interpretation component of the discussion. They should reflect the summative evaluation of the literature you have reviewed, their correlation with the study, and the findings you have reported. These conclusions and recommendations should reflect the synthesis and evaluation levels of cognition. You should inform the reader why you have drawn your conclusions and why you have made your recommendations. The conclusions and recommendations should be stated clearly and succinctly. They are your final commentary on the topic and should summarize your thinking. Generate a succinct and strong statement of what you have thought, determined, concluded, and recommended in terms of the topic you have chosen and the study you have completed. Determining is consistent with the synthesis and evaluation levels of the cognitive taxonomy and the dissemination level of the experiential taxonomy.

Again, best wishes to you as you develop your paper. Make it important to you. Your readers will sense this and will react more positively to your work whether they agree with you or choose to disagree with you. Remember that your paper is a reflection of you and your professionalism. Make it the very best that it can be. In doing this you will have a product which will bring forth a sense of personal accomplishment.

In this course, as in many courses at your university or organization, you are expected to write a formal professional paper, a professional writing project, or a quantitative or qualitative study. For some of you this may be your first experience in writing a paper of this kind. For others this may be a further experience in writing. For all, this will be an opportunity to demonstrate your skills in writing. Writing a formal paper is a challenging task, but can be done well if you begin early in the course or time frame, keep to a personal schedule, and follow the style and format adopted by your university or your organization.

This handbook has been prepared as a guide and a quick reference on how to organize your paper or your study. A section by section developmental format for writing your paper, and a notation of some of the expectations of style and format which you will follow in preparing your paper have been included. You need to remember that the style manual for your paper is the latest edition of the *Publication Manual of the American Psychological Association* (APA). Your paper will consist of the following sections: Title page, abstract, introduction, review of literature, method, results, discussion, and references. Appendixes and a bibliography, if you have them in your paper, will also be discussed. You should remember the method and results sections are included only for courses or papers requiring a quantitative or qualitative study. In some instances you may be asked to include a table of contents. The preparation of a table of contents is included as a part of this handbook in case it is expected or required.

If you are submitting a formal writing project or white paper, preparing a guidebook or handbook, planning a staff development program, evaluating a program, writing a grant proposal, doing an action research study, or preparing curriculum, you can learn how to prepare each of these in this work. We added these writing projects except one in the third edition. In this fourth edition we have added how to prepare curriculum for those responsible for writing curriculum. This section on curriculum is designed both for teachers and for anyone designated to prepare curriculum for inservices or for special training. We have added, in an appendix a format for developing curriculum. You may use it or any other format suggested by your supervisor.

You have, in this work, direction on how to prepare each of these formal documents, proposals, programs, studies, or curriculum. There are other kinds of papers you may need to prepare. You will find help in this work even though we do not discuss them in this work. The format for these other writing projects may vary somewhat, but they generally follow the formal writing style and format. In this work, you have sections such as common errors, formal writing conventions, and grammar usage you can use for reference. The format and style for most of these other kinds of papers are frequently consistent with the APA. You will find that the APA format and style are discussed throughout this work. Consult your instructor or your supervisor for specific help in writing other kinds of formal writing projects.

Every professional graduate paper will contain some or all of the sections described in this *Handbook*. Instructors or supervisors may make minor adjustments in organization, but the basic component sections of the paper will be prepared as outlined in this *Handbook*. You need to remember every section of the paper begins at the top of a new page. These notes are organized so expectations for each section of the paper are discussed sequentially. Writing tips are included at the end of the notes for each section of the paper. They are designed to help you focus on how to prepare the content of each section of your paper. In this fourth edition, we have included a model paper. You may use it as a reference for what a paper should look like. It is a model for a review of literature paper.

In the pages that follow, each section of the paper or study is discussed and described. There are differences between a quantitative or qualitative study and a review of literature paper and these differences are pointed out. Most papers written at the graduate level are reviews of literature. In only a few courses are papers requiring a research format expected. All elements of each section of formal papers and research studies are detailed in this work. Please be sure to refer to this work as you are writing your paper. You will be expected to adhere to the format and the writing style throughout your paper. In addition to the discussions about the sections of the paper, there are additional components of this work that you will need to review carefully. The first component deals with common errors found in formal papers. If you study this component when reviewing the preparation of the other sections of your work, you will be well on your way to writing a strong graduate paper, research study, or one of the programs discussed in this work. The second component of this work is a commentary on formal writing conventions. This is provided to give you, as the writer, an additional perspective on writing formal papers. It is written in narrative form and provides another component and support for your writing. The third component is an end note with a focus on strategies for building your professional skills. In this fourth edition additional components have been added. They are sections on preparing formal reports or white papers, preparing a guidebook or handbook, preparing a staff development program, preparing a program evaluation, developing grant proposals, preparing an action research study and writing curriculum. Seven appendixes are included. In Appendix A a checklists for writing each section of the paper both for review of literature papers and for research studies is included including table of contents and bibliography. It is important that you use these checklists because they provide a list of the expectations and requirements for each section of the paper or study. Page number referents for finding information about each items on the checklist are noted for each item within the checklist for that section of the paper. Appendix B has a suggested scoring rubric for formal papers. Appendix C is a suggested evaluation guide for formal papers. In Appendix D a format for presenting papers is provided. Appendix E contains a list of common references. Appendix F is a guide to developing surveys and questionnaires. Appendix G is a guide to formal grammar usage and has been augmented for this fourth edition. A glossary of terms pertaining to writing and research is included following the appendixes.

There are many additional sources for writing papers and studies which can be used. Among them are the *Publication Manual of the American Psychological Association* (American Psychological Association, 2001), Cone and Foster's work (1993), Carver (1984), Strunk and White (2000), and Turabian (1996). If you are in the field of education and need general resources, consult Darling-Hammond (1997), Eisner (1994)), Joyce and Weil with Calhoun (2004), and Reeves (2003). If you need additional resources in research use Gall, Borg, and Gall (1996), Mertens (2005), and Merriam (1998). There are, of course, many more. If you are in the business department you may wish to use, among others, Bennis (1997, 2000), Bennis and Goldsmith (2003), Drucker (1967), Howard (1993), Sample (2003), or Likert (1967). Again, there are many more resources for you to review and consult in these and other fields of study.

In this fourth edition a number of changes have been made. Additions and corrections have been made in the explanations for how to do each section of the paper. These changes have been more substantive in the method and results sections of the work. Writing tips have been extended and are more detailed. There have been additions and changes made in the section on common errors in formal papers. Additional information has been included in the section on conventions of formal writing. In the sample references appendix, additional samples have been included for writer's use. The glossary has been extended to include more terms students and writers encounter in classes or in their organizations. We have added a section on preparing curriculum and have also included a model paper. We feel that, in this fourth edition, the scope of the work has been broadened and the content, while remaining user friendly. This fourth edition has been augmented by these additions and has been reviewed for clarity, specificity, and necessary detail. Many of the changes we have made have come to us from students who have used the *Handbook*. Suggestions have also come from our colleagues. We thank them for helping to make this edition one that writers will find even more useful than the first three editions.

We wish to acknowledge the assistance and support of our colleagues, our friends, and our students for reading and critiquing this work. Their assistance and responses have been invaluable as we have prepared this document. In field tests and in reviewing the document our students have been very helpful in asking questions, helping us clarify meaning and content, and in critiquing the *Handbook* as they used it. Special thanks go to the late John W. Stallings of the University of Southern California for his support and guidance early in the development of this work. We also want to thank James Mbuva of National University for his review of the manuscript and for his support in making it better and more complete. We want to thank Marilyn Koeller and Lorraine Leavitt, our colleagues, for their encouragement and help. Especially, however, we want to thank our families. Their patience, their support and their love have meant much to us. Finally we want to thank the following: Dr. Natalia Bilan, Dr. Joseph R. Ruggio, and Dr. Richard A. Ott, without whom this work could not have been completed.

The purpose of this work was to briefly explicate the format, organization, and style of formal papers for students. The *Publication Manual of the American Psychological Association* was the format adopted by many universities and organizations. This work was consistent with that manual. It was designed as a guide for students and others when writing formal papers. Five steps in writing a professional paper were included in the preface. Each section of the paper including title page, abstract, introduction, review of literature, method, results, discussion, references, and table of contents were addressed. Sections on how to prepare formal papers and white papers, guidebooks, staff development programs, program evaluation, grant proposals, action research, and curriculum have been included. Writing tips were included for each section. Conventions of formal writing were included. There were also discussions on common errors, grammar, and notes on building professional skills. Sections on grammar, writing formal papers, evaluating programs, writing funding proposals, and doing action research were included. Checklists for each section were included in an appendix.

1

Preparing the Title Page

The title page is the first page of the paper and contains the following elements: Page header, running head, title, author, and author's affiliation. Nothing more than this information needs to be included on the title page of the paper. This is what the American Psychological Association manual requires. Be sure that the American Psychological Association (APA) style and format for this page are followed. If your professor, instructor, or supervisor has additional requirements, you should include them as part of your title page.

Page Header

The page header appears on the title page and every page of the paper including the abstract, reference section and appendixes. The page header consists of the first two words or two important words of the title of the paper and the sequential number of the page.

The number and the second word of the page header are separated by a tab space of five to seven spaces. The page header is justified to the right margin. It is the only element of your paper that has a right margin justification. The page header is always located on the top right hand side of the paper on the first print line. The page header is how you number the

> The title page is the first page of the paper and contains the following elements: Page header, running head, title, author, and author's affiliation.

pages of your paper. Do not use numbers at the bottom of the page or just the number at the top of the page. Each page of the paper including references, bibliography, and appendixes must have a page header with the page numbers in sequential order. The title page is page one of the paper. The rationale for this is that the pages are submitted and read by the reviewer in loose leaf order. If there is a mixup of the pages, the page header serves to help reorder the pages.

Running Head

The running head is placed on the title page one double space below the page header and is justified to the left margin. The *r* in running head is capitalized. The *h* in head is not capitalized. The words running head are followed by a colon. Following the colon, is the running head which is simply a short version of your full title not to exceed 50 characters. All letters in all words of the running head are in capital letters. There is a specific purpose for the running head. You are writing a professional paper that is suitable for publication. The running head you have selected tells the reviewer and the editor what you would like to use as the header for each page of your article or paper when it is published. This is also how your paper will be referred to in professional discussions and in some bibliographies and abstracts. The running head appears only on the title page of your paper.

Title

The full title of your paper is centered mid page. The first letter of each word of the title is capitalized except for articles and prepositions. If the title is lengthy, it should be divided appropriately into two lines with the second line being justified and centered under the first line. Do not use acronyms in your title. Write out the acronym. Do not use italics, abbreviations, or quotations marks in your title. Your title is a descriptor of your paper or study. Make it clear and concise.

Author

One double space below the title is your name. Your name is centered and justified with the title. Do not use the word by. For two authors, separate the names of the authors with the word and. Names should be placed on one line, space permitting. For three or more authors separate the names by a comma. Before the last author is listed use the word and. Authors names, if necessary, can be placed on two or more lines with the names centered and justified under the title.

Author's Affiliation

This is the university affiliation or professional affiliation of the author. In most cases the affiliation will be the university in which you are enrolled or the organization of which you are a member. If you are submitting this paper for publication you may use the university, your school district, or your professional affiliation. The affiliation notation is centered one double space below the author's name. No other information appears on the title page. Do not put date, course title, course number, instructor's name, or any other information on the title page unless required by the professor, the instructor, or your supervisor.

Writing Tips

Be sure to follow the format explicitly. The title page is the first page the reader examines. It should reflect the information needed. The page header must be justified on the right margin at the top of the page. Ensure that the title, your name, and your affiliation are centered at mid page. Count the spaces if necessary. Select the running head carefully; it is a shorter version of your title. The running head is justified on the left. Do not use acronyms, italics, abbreviations, or quotation marks in the title or in the running head. Remember that the running head is written with all capital letters and is one double space below the page header. Make the title of your paper clear, cogent, and concise.

For a quick review of all the required components of the title page refer to the checklist for the title page in Appendix A on page 109. The use of this checklist will ensure that you have included all the necessary components of the title page in your paper.

2

Preparing the Table of Contents

Chapter

A table of contents is not included in most formal papers because they tend to be relatively short. For longer papers and manuscripts such as this *Handbook*, a table of contents can be very helpful. A table of contents may also be required by your instructor or supervisor. Tables of content are included immediately following the title page. Tables of contents are numbered in lower case Roman numerals as is the preface if one is included. Roman numerals are used only for the table of contents and any preface or prefatory remarks. The introduction are usually numbered in lower case Roman numerals

Lower case Roman numerals, as noted, are used in the table of contents and are numbered on the same line as the page header one tab space from the last letter of the page header. The page header is justified to the right margin. The title of the section, table of contents, is centered one double space below the page header. The name of each section or chapter of the work is entered on a line beginning one double space below the table of contents title. A dotted line with one space between each dot completes the line to the page number which is justified on the right. Each succeeding section is listed one double space below the preceding section. When categories are included, they must be indented one tab space on the line below the section title. There must be at least two categories when they are listed. This pattern continues until all sections and categories are noted by page numbers. Page numbers are provided for each section, category,

Tables of content are included immediately following the title page.

5

and subcategory. The page numbers are justified on the right margin. If your paper has subcategories, they are indented two tab spaces from the left margin or one tab space more than categories. If you have subcategories in your table of contents there must be at least two.

Writing Tips

Preparing a table of contents must be done accurately and carefully. Be sure that you have one space between each dot on the line from the end of the title of that section, category, or subcategory to the number of the page. Remember that page numbers are justified on the right. Use Arabic numbers only, except for the notation of the preface. Categories are indented one tab space and are entered on the line below the section or chapter title. There must be at least two category titles when they are used. If you have subcategories, they are indented and entered two double spaces from the left margin or one tab space more than categories. There must be at least two subcategory titles entered when they are used. Just a word on prefaces and prefatory remarks. Prefaces are not included in short papers or research studies and if they are, they serve to introduce the work, to illustrate its organization, and to acknowledge those who assisted you and supported you during the development of the work. Do not include any prefatory comments unless specifically asked to do so by your instructor or supervisor.

For a quick review of the expected elements of the table of contents, refer to the checklist in Appendix A page 110. The use of this checklist will help ensure that you have completed the required components of the table of contents.

3 Preparing the Abstract

Chapter

The abstract is page two of your paper. An abstract, as a model, is included on page two of this work. The abstract has a page header numbered as page two of the paper. Below the page header is the word abstract which is centered one double space below the page header. The a in abstract is capitalized, none of the other letters in the word is capitalized. The purpose of the abstract is to inform the reader very succinctly about the purpose of your paper, the parameters of the topic included in the paper, and the pertinence or importance of the paper in the field. You should also note salient points you have found in your review of literature. If you have written a research study you will state the problem or question you investigated as part or all of the purpose of the paper. Your findings, conclusions, and recommendations are also included. Readers will choose to read your paper or not to read your paper based on what you include in the abstract. The abstract thus becomes the most important part of your paper in terms of how many people read your paper. It must be very carefully written.

The APA limits the abstract to no more than 960 characters or about 120 words. In some instances instructors or supervisors may allow you up to 150 words. Readers are interested in a quick overview of your paper. Any additional words could deter from the purpose of the abstract which is to inform reviewers and readers and

The purpose of the abstract is to inform the reader very succinctly about the purpose of your paper, the parameters of the topic included in the paper, and the pertinence or importance of the paper in the field.

to cause them to be interested in your work. In order to conserve words use no citations and be as succinct as possible. At the same time, however, be very specific about the content, conclusions, and recommendations of your paper.

The abstract is not indented. It is blocked. It consists of one paragraph with all lines justified only on the left margin of the paper. Right margins are not justified in the abstract, nor are they justified on the right margin anywhere in the paper except for the page header and the page numbers in the table of contents. The narrative of the paragraph begins one double space below the word abstract. All narrative lines are double spaced. Do not break words at the end of a line. No line should end with a hyphen. A good abstract is accurate, concise, and specific. You report what the paper was about and include in the abstract salient points from your review of literature, your findings, your conclusions, and your recommendations. The abstract is not evaluative. No personal opinions or statements can or should be included. The conclusions and recommendations which should be included in the abstract are the nearest you can come to expressing your ideas or perspectives and even these should retain a non evaluative tenor.

Abstracts are written in the past or present perfect tense. The opening sentences define the purpose of the paper or the issues studied in your paper. These sentences identify the parameters and limitations of the paper and its importance to the field. The next few sentences emphasize the major points from the review of literature as well as notations on your method and your findings if you have done a research study. In the last few sentences of the abstract summarize your conclusions and recommendations.

The abstract is the last section of the paper that is written. You usually complete the introduction, review of literature, the method, the results, and the discussion sections before writing the abstract. Once you have completed the paper and understand clearly the scope, sequence, and findings of your work, you can then write the abstract with more clarity, precision, and focus. Write clearly and concisely using simple sentences so that the reader can quickly gain insight into the topic of your paper, its purpose, its parameters, what you learned about the topic, your findings, and your conclusions and recommendations. Avoid citations and acronyms in the abstract because they count as words and thus decrease the number of words you can use to tell the reader what needs to be understood about the paper.

When your paper has been published the abstract may appear as the initial introduction or paragraph of your paper in the journal of publication. It may or may not be noted as the abstract. Abstracts are also published in various professional publications such as Educational Resources Information Center (ERIC) and APA Psychological Abstracts.

Writing Tips

Be sure to keep to the word limitation of 120 to 150 words. Your abstract is written in the past or present perfect tense. Eliminate any unnecessary words or phrases. Use short simple sentences as much as possible. Do not use acronyms in the abstract. Avoid using adjectives and adverbs as much as possible. Use technical terms and language only if they are absolutely necessary. Do not include citations. Remember to include conclusions and recommendations. These are generally included in the last sentence or sentences of the abstract. In a research study you should include the question or issue you studied. You need to note whether it was a quantitative or qualitative study or a combinations of both major kinds of studies. You will also need to include a summary statement of the findings or the results of your study.

For a quick review of the expected elements of the abstract refer to the checklist for abstracts in Appendix A on page 111. The use of this checklist will help ensure that you have included all expected components of the abstract in your paper.

4 Preparing the Introduction

The introduction is the first narrative section of your paper. It is noted on the page header as page three of your paper. You center the full title of your paper one double space below the page header. If you need two lines for the title of your paper use them. Be sure the second line of the title is centered one double space below the first line of the title. All first letters in the words of the title are capitalized except for articles and prepositions. Do not title this section introduction.

In the introduction there are three basic components. First, you define the purpose of the paper. If you are writing a research study you need to include in your purpose the question or issue you are studying. Second, you establish the importance of the topic in the field of study. Third, you provide a rationale for choosing the topic and for your interest in the topic. Nothing more is necessary for inclusion in the introduction.

Purpose of Paper

In defining the purpose of your paper you provide only as much information as is necessary. The purpose or purposes can be written in a few sentences or, depending on the topic, can be slightly longer. Make sure the reader has a clear understanding of the purpose of the paper, how you have defined it, and its limitations. If

> *Your reader should understand the purpose of the paper, why it is important, and why you have an interest in the topic.*

your problem or topic has many components or facets you will need to define the parameters of your paper carefully and make sure that the focus is clearly stated and specific. You may also include the issue or question being reviewed or studied. The reader needs to understand the purpose at the beginning of the paper. Make your purpose clear and provide as much information as you need to provide the reader with a clear and concise presentation of your purpose in writing the paper.

If you are preparing a quantitative or qualitative study, you will need to clearly define the question or the issue and the variables being studied in the purpose of your research. You may also need to include some information on population and process as well as on data collection instruments and how they were evaluated. This information must be briefly stated and provide enough information for the reader to clearly understand the focus, limitations, and parameters of the study. In writing your statement of purpose, you need to make it concise, clear, and cogent and provide as much information you feel the reader needs. In many instances you are writing within a specified time frame or deadline so your topic or purpose must be something you can develop well within the time frame under which you are working. Your first paragraph or few paragraphs of the introduction should make the purpose of the paper clear to the reader and provide the reader with a focused purpose for the paper as well as its parameters and limitations.

Importance of Topic

After you have written your purpose statement, you have the obligation to emphasize the importance of the topic. Remember that the work you are preparing is a professional paper or research study and needs to evidence a substantive contribution to the field. In this component of the introduction you will briefly bring forward issues that will be reviewed in your paper and develop a background for the reader so that the topic and the issues within it are recognized as important to the profession. This background of information should be defined and prepared with clarity and with evidence to support it. You should discuss briefly the literature you have reviewed and cite only salient points from your review. You do not go into great detail in the introduction because you will do this in your review of literature. In the introduction you are defining and describing, not going into detail. Your review of literature will be organized around categories and subcategories of your topic and will provide the detail needed. You may want to organize this part of the introduction around those categories, though this is not mandatory nor is it essential in establishing the importance of the topic. You will need to use some citations in this section, but do not go into an exhaustive review of literature. As the writer you cannot establish the importance of the topic. The importance is established only by the sources, authors, and researchers you cite. Touch only on the pertinent and seminal sources that emphasize the importance of the topic, the question, or the issues. Do only enough so that the reader understands the importance of the topic and has a good grasp of the background of the topic as well as the limitations and parameters of the paper. The reader should know not only the subject of the paper and its importance, but also know the specific issues and topics that are the focus of your paper as well as some of the resources you discuss within the review of literature.

Rationale for Choosing Topic

To provide closure in the introduction you will want to identify the rationale or your reason for selecting this topic. Let the reader know why you are doing the paper or the study and why you have an interest in the issues or questions discussed in your paper. Your choice can come from a personal need to learn more about the topic. It can come from a feeling that exploring the area and studying it will help you become professionally more competent. Your choice can also be made because this topic has within it issues that are pertinent in your school district or workplace. The rationale for a research study could be the need to test a theory, an intervention, or to determine attitudes and perspectives about an issue or a problem. There could also be other professional reasons. You define your reasons and state them succinctly and to the point. Do not go into great detail. Completing the rationale closes the introduction.

Writing Tips

It is important to remember to write the introduction in a non evaluative style. You do not reveal any biases, predetermined expectations, or outcomes at this point in the paper. Your writing should reflect your professional interest in the topic and a recognition that it is important to you and to the profession. Everything in this section is written in the past tense or present perfect tense except for direct quotes. This is very important and you should review what you have written to correct any tense as well as other syntactic issues. One of the most common errors for those who are just beginning the process of writing formal papers is syntax. Avoid compound and complex sentences as much as possible though they may occasionally be necessary. Write clearly and use short simple sentences consistently to ensure clarity, cogency, and continuity. Say only what needs to be said and use an economy of expression. Keep in mind that "brevity is the soul of wit." Alexander Pope was correct. You can write with clarity, cogency, and develop continuity through saying only what needs to be said briefly. In doing this you can effectively retain interest and involvement by the reader. Your reader should understand the purpose of the paper, why it is important, and why you have an interest in the topic. This is most important and you need to ensure that these are included in the paper. Sometimes writers include a transitional paragraph after the three components have been finished. While this is not necessary, it can give the reader an understanding of what is coming next in the paper and how the remaining sections are organized. This paragraph, if it is included, is generally brief, but may help the reader make a smooth transition from the introduction to the review of literature and a clear picture of how you have organized the paper. Finally, do not use superscript or subscript in your paper unless it is a scientific or mathematical formula or is approved for usage by the APA.

For a quick review of the expected elements of the introduction refer to the checklist for the introduction in Appendix A on page 112. The use of this checklist will help you ensure that you have included all the necessary components of the introduction in your paper.

5 Preparing the Review of Literature

This section of your paper or study follows the introduction and is called the review of literature. This section is a major professional component of your paper. It also provides the foundation for information and commentary about your topic. It is titled review of literature. The review of literature begins on a separate page with the title centered one double space below the page header. The review of literature is almost always the longest and most detailed section of your paper and informs the reader about the literature you have reviewed. It provides your report on the issues and content of the literature reviewed. The review of literature includes only sources that are pertinent to your paper. Your review of literature also provides an evidentiary base for your conclusions and recommendations. If you are writing a quantitative or qualitative research study, the review of literature not only provides an evidentiary base for the question or issue you are studying or testing, but in addition, provides the reader with a review of concurrent and corollary research in the field.

The review of literature is generally organized with an introductory paragraph, categories delineating major areas of focus within the review, and sometimes with subcategories within the broader categories. The introductory paragraph serves as an organizational content design for your paper and should be brief and clearly written. In some instances a closing paragraph may be included, even though it is not generally necessary in most papers.

> The review of literature is generally organized with an introductory paragraph, categories delineating major areas of focus within the review, and sometimes with subcategories within the broader categories.

Introductory Paragraph

The introductory paragraph of the review of literature is generally relatively brief and contains only information about how the review of literature is organized. You will name the categories in the sequence in which they appear in the review. Names of categories and subcategories are not capitalized unless they are proper nouns or are the first word following a colon. If you include categories that have subcategories, you will name the subcategories immediately following the naming of the category. Subcategories are necessary when they help you focus on specific information within a larger category. There must be at least two categories within the paper. Likewise, there must be at least two subcategories within each category where they are used. The names of the categories should be brief; usually one or two words and seldom more than three or four words. In a qualitative or quantitative study, you will follow the same content guidelines for your introductory paragraph. The categories should relate directly to research in the area of study as well as related categories pertinent to your study. Do not provide any other information in the introductory paragraph. The sole purpose of the paragraph is to inform the reader about the organization of the review of literature. It is, in a sense, a table of contents for the review of literature. Immediately following the opening paragraph, the title of the first category is provided. The title of each category is on a separate line, is justified on the left margin, and is in italics.

Categories

A category in your review of literature helps you organize your review into logical areas of focus and that are defined areas of emphasis. Using categories helps the writer organize findings and information for the review in terms of identified components of the paper as noted in the purpose of the paper and stated in the introduction. Categories also help the reader to focus on specific information related to the content of the category. Each category needs to relate to the purpose of the paper or study as you have defined it in the introduction. The name of each category is on a separate line and is written in italics one double space below the narrative line above. Every word in the category is capitalized except for articles and prepositions. The name of the category is justified on the left margin. The narrative begins on the next line.

When writing about your findings, you must be objective. No personal opinions, biases, or interpretations can be expressed in the review of literature. Avoid value words when writing the review. Let the researchers, the authors, and commentators speak for themselves. You can paraphrase their works and use direct quotes, but you do not comment on them. Your comments are reserved for the interpretation component of the discussion section of your paper. You should write the review of literature in the past tense or the present perfect tense with the exception of direct quotes where the author may use the present or future tense. Remember every resource you have reviewed has already been written and published in some context. If there are differing views among the researchers or writers within a particular category you should indicate this, but without personal comment or interpretation. Direct quotes require citations and page numbers. Quotes of forty or more words must be blocked. To block a quotation indent every line of the quotation one tab space and do not use quotation marks. All blocked quotes are double spaced. If you paraphrase a researcher's or author's work, you must provide a citation. Indeed, every time you bring new information to the attention of the reader there must be a citation. Every paragraph including new information must have one or more citations. You must follow APA style and format for all citations.

You should go into as much detail as necessary when you are reviewing an article, a book, a document, internet material, visual material, or other resource. Through the material you have reviewed you are presenting information about the topic for the reader and providing an evidentiary basis for your interpretation, findings, conclusions, and recommendations. These become part of the discussion section of the paper. You are also demonstrating the importance of your sources in the field and their relationship to the paper or to the study. You need to provide a clear understanding of how the resources relate to the category in which they are cited. How the resources relate to the topic and to what the authors presented in their articles, books, or studies is essential. It is important that the citations and quotations be consistent in content with the context of the category and the topic. In the review of literature you provide the reader with the information you have determined to be pertinent in explicating the issues, questions, or problems you have defined as the focus and purpose of your paper or study.

Subcategories

Subcategories are component parts of a category. You must have at least two subcategories in each category to justify their use. Subcategories provide for more specific areas of focus or component parts of the category in which they appear. You have more organizational flexibility when you use subcategories. For example, if your category is teaching strategies, in each subcategory you can focus on one of the identified strategies chosen for review. Subcategories follow the same organization and writing style as categories. Titles of subcategories should be no more than two or three words. The title of each subcategory is written in italics. It is indented one tab space and is followed by a period. The narrative begins immediately following the title of the subcategory on the same line as the title of the subcategory. Only the first word of the subcategory and proper nouns are capitalized.

Closing Paragraph

A closing paragraph is infrequently included, but if your review is lengthy or you wish to recapitulate the organization, you can include this paragraph. The only purpose of this paragraph is to again remind the reader what you have done in the review of literature. You simply rename the categories and subcategories to remind the reader what you have included in your review of literature. You do not introduce new information or use citations. You write your closing paragraph without personal commentary or interpretation. That is reserved for the discussion section of the paper. In most instances this paragraph is not needed, but if you feel the need to include it, please do so.

Writing Tips

The review of literature is usually the longest section of your paper. It is written in narrative form and must follow the APA format and style. Clarity of expression and logical continuity are important elements of writing. Use an economy of expression. Say only what needs to be said. Use simple sentences most of the time. Compound and complex sentences should be avoided, unless needed for explanation or clarification. Avoid the use of jargon, buzz words, and overuse of professional terminology. Do not use colloquialisms, idioms, or slang expressions in your paper. You are writing a formal paper. You are writing for an audience of your peers and they read the paper with similar professional backgrounds and experiences.

Your review of literature should be written in the past or present perfect tense except for direct quotes. Whenever you introduce new information to the reader, you must cite the source of that information. If you use a direct quote, you must cite the source and the page number. Use quotation marks at the beginning and end of direct quotes of less than forty words. Direct quotes of forty or more words must be blocked. You do not use quotation marks with blocked quotes. If a blocked quote has a quotation within it, use an apostrophe to show that quotation. Do not use superscript or subscript except in certain mathematical or scientific formulae as defined within the APA *Manual*.

You should predominantly use the active voice in your writing. Be very careful to eliminate any anthropomorphisms. Remember that research cannot tell nor report, neither can articles or books say. Only researchers and authors can tell, report, write, or say. Even in this day of political correctness, there should be agreement of subject and verb as well as in personal pronouns. Avoid the use of he/she even though in a very few cases it may be unavoidable. Sentences, if they are well crafted, can for the most part, be written without using he/she. Make sure the reader understands the referent when you use a personal pronoun. When referring to people use who or whom. When referring to animals or inanimate objects use that or which. While there are certain well defined conventions for formal writing, they must be followed. At the same time you should strive to make your paper lively and interesting to the reader.

Simplicity and continuity create a more fluent paper where meaning is more easily understood. You can go into as much detail as is necessary through a simple, straightforward, cogent style. Strive to make your review of literature reflect this kind of narrative flow. Be sure also to edit and carefully review this section of your paper or study. This is important in order to make sure that your review of literature is consistent with the purpose of your paper. Your review of literature provides an evidentiary base for your conclusions and recommendations. The review of literature should also reflect the content necessary to ensure that the reader clearly understands the scope and sequence of the resources you have reviewed and how they pertain to your topic. Be sure that everything in the review of literature is double spaced.

For a review of the elements necessary to the review of literature refer to the checklist for the review of literature in Appendix A on page 113. The use of the checklist will ensure that you have included all the components of a review of literature in your paper.

6

Preparing the Method Section

Chapter

A method section is included only in papers when you are doing a qualitative or quantitative research study. In a research study the method section immediately follows the review of literature. Almost all other formal papers are referred to as review of literature papers. Some undergraduate and graduate classes require a research study. If you are doing a research study and need to include a method section you must include the following categories: Question or issue being studied, limitations of the study, variables, population, sample size, time frame, process, data collection, data analysis, and assessment and evaluation. In some instances there may be some redundancy, but in each category there is a defined focus with the need to present the information from a specific perspective. Research studies can be either quantitative or qualitative.

Quantitative studies are experimental, empirical, positivist and statistical. The focus of quantitative studies is on prediction, attitudes and perceptions, confirmation, and the testing of interventions or hypotheses. The analysis is deductive and the findings are precise and numerical. Qualitative studies focus on the nature and the essence of groups of people. They involve case studies, fieldwork, ethnography, and phenomenology. The goal of a qualitative investigation is understanding the beliefs and attitudes of a group, the structure of identified phenomena, constructivist methodology, and generating grounded theory. The mode of analysis is inductive and the findings are comprehensive and richly descriptive.

> A method section is included only in papers when you are doing a qualitative or quantitative research study.

You need to determine which of these approaches to research would be more appropriate for your study. In some instances a study could include both kinds of research approaches. Each of the categories in a research study is given below with a brief description of the content that should be included in each category. The title of each category is italicized and on a separate line from the text as shown below.

Question or Issue

The questions or issues you are studying are the core purposes of your paper. You stated them as part of the purpose in the introduction to your paper and you need to restate them at the very beginning of your method section. In this section of the paper you need to clarify for the reader the issues and questions motivating the study as well as specific variables being tested. You delimit the area of study within the identified questions or issues noted. You need to be very specific here so that the reader clearly understands what you are studying and how you have focused your particular study. These initial statements of the question or issue are key to the method section of your paper and need to be very carefully done. In this category of the method section you are delimiting the scope of the paper and defining its parameters. Craft it so there is no ambiguity about what your questions or issues are and how you are framing them. You also need to note the specific focus of the study. You are stating the purpose of the research, the questions or issues studied, and the variables tested. You are also defining as the limitations of the study. You may need also to include briefly some information on the population, measures used, process, and analyses of the date even though these will be more fully developed later. Here they simply provide a very brief overview of the study and are included for clarity of understanding the nature of the study.

Limitations

There has never been a study that is totally complete and without flaw. Every research study has limitations and defined parameters. You need to point out some of those limitations in the study you are doing. Among those limitations could be the size of the population and whether they volunteered, were a convenience sample, or were selected at random. Limitations could also be areas of information or the variables that you are studying or those variables that you are not studying. Limitations can be the time frame for completing the study. Limitations help the reader understand what you are not including in the study and what the constraints of the study imply for your work. Limitations can also be resources, funds, and materials available. Limitations could further include the kind of instruments selected for gathering and analyzing data. Other limitations could include variables studied, resources, and personnel. In this section you need to make clear to the reader how each of these limitations affected the study or related to the outcomes.

Variables

In any research paper there are many variables that could be studied. The demographic data gathered in a survey, questionnaire, or interview can help you identify the variables. An intervention or a treatment to be used with a group can constitute a variable. In this category of the method section you list the variables you plan to test in the study. You may also note some variables you are not testing. Variable definition is exceptionally important both to you and to your readers. Each component element you are testing or studying could be a variable. You need to know and your readers need to know very specifically and definitionally the variables that are being tested within the study. The definition of variables should provide, for the reader, a clear and concise statement of what you are studying or what you are testing. Some research studies fail because the variables tested are not clearly defined. Variables should have a clear and direct relationship to the purpose of the study. Sometimes you may be working with only one variable, but often two or more variables are involved in the study. You may want to focus on the expected outcomes for the identified variables and interpret the projected outcomes for their impact on the population. If you do this the variables need to be noted. You will provide details and interpretation in the results and discussion sections of the study. You can also note related variables not included in the study. You need to include all these items in the variable category of your method section.

Population

Who you are studying is also very important. You identify the population studied in this category of the method section. Populations vary in terms of the kind of study in which you are involved. Quantitative studies usually, but not always, require both a control and experimental group. These two groups need to be as equally matched as possible. Quantitative studies can also include a population responding to surveys, questionnaires, or interviews. Qualitative studies generally require only one group. Population size can vary according to the nature of the study. If you are doing a single case study your population is one person. If you are doing a large quantitative study your population could be hundreds or even thousands. If you are doing a lengthy or longitudinal study, you need to account for an attrition of members of the identified population. You must define age group, characteristics, gender, commonalities, and differences. You need to provide the reader information on how you selected the population and why they were selected. Note whether they were selected randomly or were a convenience population. Note any criteria used for selection of the population. These criteria could be experience, achievement, specific skills, or other identified personality or behavioral attributes. Do this notation clearly and succinctly for your readers. Make sure the readers clearly understand how the population was selected, why it was selected, and the criteria used for their selection. It is important for your readers to know this if they wish to replicate the study.

Sampling Process

This could be a separate category in the method section of your study, or it could be included within the population category subsection. You may break this out as a separate section if you need to describe in detail your sampling strategies and procedures. Here you need to provide a rationale for the size of the population, how the population is selected, and why it is limited to the particular size you chose. You may need to justify the size of the population in terms of why it is not larger or smaller. Sample size information could also include details about any subgroups within the population and how they might relate to variables being tested. You may also need to note the kind of sampling techniques used in selecting your population. You may, for example, need to note variances in achievement, experience, or skills as being subgroups in the population. The use of sample size as a separate subcategory in the method section of the paper allows you to do a more detailed description of the nature of the population in terms of subgroups within it and in terms of variables tested. You need to note how you chose your sample. Note whether it was a random selection or a convenience sample. Other sampling strategies used also need to be addressed in this category. This kind of information could also help frame the selection and definition of the variables studied.

Time Frame

Here you simply provide the reader with the time frame for the study. Within this time frame you may want to note the sequence of activities and events in the study such as pre and post tests, as well as points of emphasis and benchmarks at specific times during the study. The category on the time frame can include information such as when and how data are collected, when data are analyzed, and when the final report of the study will be ready for presentation or publication. A time frame is not only the beginning time and ending time, it is a catalogue and sequence of activities and events within the time frame. The time frame will help keep you on task and oriented toward an appropriate sequence of activities within the time frame. It will also keep the reader informed about the time sequence in which the study was done and the activities and events involved therein. If the reader wishes to replicate the study, the specifics of the time frame can be very helpful.

 ## Process

In this category of the method section you tell the reader how you did the study. You list the steps and sequence of activities. In a quantitative study you note the pre and posttests and the nature of the intervention or treatment. In a qualitative study you note your observations, interviews and and review of documents. You indicate how you coded the data from them. For both kinds of research study you explain the process in a step by step sequential manner. You need to be careful to note each of the sequential steps and discuss each step briefly. If you expect problems with at any activity or step within the process, be sure to mention them. Your purpose in this part of the method section is to delineate the formative process and make it clear to the reader. In effect, this is a brief overview of the study and how it was accomplished. This category of the method section can also include brief statements about how the data were gathered, analyzed, and evaluated. A more explicit discussion of these topics comes later in the method section, but for the reader to understand the process, you will want to briefly note them.

In any study there are formative processes and summative processes. The formative process is as important as the summative findings of the study if the study is to be replicated or the findings implemented. In this category of the method section your direct focus on the formative process. You need to relate the formative process to the summative outcomes briefly in this category of the method section of the paper. When the readers finish this category of the method section of the paper, they should have a clear understanding of how you completed the study, the steps within the process, issues and problems within the steps, and the linkage of that process to the summative outcomes.

Data Collection

How you collect the data is essential information for the reader. You need to include, in this category, information on the instruments you used in your study. You need to tell about the tests, questionnaires, observations, surveys, interviews, document reviews, and any other measures you used to gather data on your population and on the variables tested. Instruments and other measures used need to be described and made clear to the reader. These measures will be different in qualitative and quantitative studies. In qualitative studies the researcher is the primary instrument. You generally use interviews, observations, and document reviews including historical documents.

You need to explain how you coded the responses in terms of the variables studied. In many cases these responses will be in coded narrative form. In quantitative studies you use tests, scales, surveys, questionnaires, completion of projects, or reports. Some studies combine both kinds of research. If you wish your readers to see your instruments or measures in their totality, they can be included in an appendix. Your obligation in the method section of the paper is to ensure that the reader understands what measures you used and how you gathered the information. The process of data collection needs to be clearly stated. You may need to comment on how it was categorized and stored. You may need to establish the validity and reliability of your measures if they are expected or required. This is particularly necessary if you have developed your own instruments and if you are doing a quantitative study.

Data Analysis

Your task in this part of the method section is to define the methods, measures, and processes used to analyze the data you have collected. If you are doing a quantitative study or are involved in an experimental, empirical, and statistical study, you will be using scales, tests, surveys, and questionnaires for gathering your data. You need to define the statistical analyses used whether they be descriptive statistical measures, correlational statistical measures, inferential statistical measures, or a combination of these statistical measures. If you are using descriptive statistical analyses you may be using mean, median, mode, average mean gain, range, and standard deviation. If you are using inferential statistical measures the most commonly used are the t test and chi square to measure for significance although there are many other inferential measures. You may use the Pearson r or other measures for correlational analyses. There are many statistical measures available for analysis of data. You need to select those most appropriate for your study.

If you are doing a qualitative study, you are focusing on the nature or essence of the population in terms of the variables tested. You need to identify how you coded materials gathered data, identified recurrent patterns, commonalities, and differences, including how you analyzed and examined those data and generalizations. This is usually done in a detailed narrative form in qualitative studies. You will, in addition, need to relate how the study evolved during its duration. You will need to determine if any grounded or substantive theory emerged from the study. You, as the researcher, are the primary instrument in data collection. These are the expectations your reader can have in this part of the method section in qualitative studies.

Assessment and Evaluation

You have finished your category on data analysis. In terms of assessment and evaluation you discuss the formative and summative processes in terms of their generalizability, their replication, and their application to other similar populations or even different populations. You may also need to address how the final report will be prepared and to whom it is to be addressed and distributed. You have the obligation in this part of the method section to bring the process together in a final statement about the study and what it means. You need here to describe both the formative and summative processes in terms of how the study progressed and what the issues and problems were that arose during the process. This is particularly important for qualitative studies and needs to be included in the narrative. The assessment and evaluation component is not a statement of findings, but is your final statement about the study itself. It is the summary of the process both formative and summative of how you arrived at your findings.

Writing Tips

The writing style of the method section is the same as it is in the other sections of your study. You seek for clarity and a cogent presentation of the narrative. You need to include enough detail so that the reader clearly understands the content of each of the categories. You should also remember that everything in the method section is written in the past tense or in the present perfect tense. This section is more technical in some respects than the introduction and review of literature and you should pay close attention to the information you present and how you present it. This section usually contains terminology that is specific to the study and statistical terms that are not always reader friendly. You should, therefore, write in simple sentences with an economy of expression, carefully wrought syntax, and with a studied clarity. Verbosity, as you know, is the last refuge of mediocrity. You are writing for your peers, but even so, you may need to explain some terms that are specific to your study. You will also be using more professional terminology in this section than in the previous sections. Make sure the technical terminology is in context and is made as clear as possible to the reader. Some of your categories in this method section may be relatively brief.

Make sure, however, that all the information needed is presented in a sequential and logical manner. Your obligation is to ensure the writing fully expresses the nature of the study and the logical development of the process you used in conducting the study. Write without personal commentary. You simply report how the study was done. This is the essence of the writing process for this section of your paper.

For a quick review of the elements necessary to this section of your paper refer to the checklist for the method section in Appendix A on page 115. Use this checklist to ensure that you have included all the expected components of the method section.

7

Preparing the Results

In the results section, when it is required, you report your findings based on the data you have collected. In the method section, you have noted how the data were collected, what instruments were used and what statistical measures or qualitative analyses were used. In the results section, you report on the outcomes of those analyses. You present or describe only the specific findings you have discovered. You do nothing more. Implications, conclusions, and recommendations are reserved for the discussion section of the study. There are two kinds of research studies which are discussed in this work. One is a quantitative study and the second is a qualitative study. Some researchers may use both in a single study. Each of these kinds of research study requires a different sequence and content for the results section and for the researcher/writer. The sequences for each kind of study are presented below.

Quantitative Results

In quantitative studies you are presenting a study based on a statistical analysis of the data collected. In your method section you identified the population, the variables to be tested, the instruments you used, and the statistical measures used to analyze the data. You will need to briefly review this information for the results section of your study. Once this is done, you

In organizing the results you need to consider the variables being tested and how best to report results in terms of those variables.

present the results. If your study is experimental you are reporting how the intervention or treatment impacted the experimental group compared to the control group who did not use the treatment or the intervention. This can be done through reporting descriptive statistical results, correlational statistical results, or inferential statistical results. You may find that you need to use more than one of these statistical approaches in your analysis of results. Descriptive measures are used to determine mean, median, mode, range, average mean gain, and standard deviation. Inferential statistical measures are used to determine significance. The most common measures used for inferential statistical analyses are the t test and chi square. If you are using a pre test-post test as your instruments to obtain results, questions of reliability and validity may arise. Be sure, whenever necessary, to respond to those questions with the data the readers expect. Correlational statistical analyses are used to show relationships among or between variables. Correlational studies are either predictive or relational and are used to establish a correlational coefficient between or among the variables used. One common correlation measure used for analysis is the Pearson product-moment coefficient or Pearson r. You need to choose the statistical measures pertinent to your study. Some formal studies are based on descriptive statistical analysis, but most researchers use other measures while at times also using descriptive statistics as well. Think through what you are studying and then determine the statistical measures appropriate to that study. In organizing the results you need to consider the variables being tested and how best to report results in terms of those variables. You can report which variable results were more significant than others, but with no personal commentary. Descriptive statistical analyses are relatively easy to do, but are not as powerful as correlational statistical analyses or inferential statistical analyses. Many graduate students use descriptive statistical measures particularly if the time frame for the study is narrow. If, however, you are going to report significance or lack of significance in your quantitative study you will need to use inferential statistical analyses. If you are reporting how variables correlated with others you use correlational analyses. In both of these statistical analyses you will need to report the level of confidence or significance of the results. These results can be shown through figures or tables included in the narrative. They may also be placed in an appendix. In this section of your work, only the results should be reported. There must be no personal commentary, interpretation, or conclusions about the results. Here you report only on the outcomes and results of your statistical analyses. These are the final results of what you have done and what happened through your study. This section needs to be a cogently and clearly written part of your paper.

Reporting Variables

When you are reporting your findings about individual variables you should identify the variable and then provide the results of your analyses of that variable. This is important to do this because the reader needs to know for which variable or variables you are providing results. Each variable represents, in most cases, data that can be disaggregated according to the demographics of the population involved in the study. Use as much detail as is necessary. The reader will need to know precisely what you have found. The reader needs to know this both in terms of the totality of the data and in terms of data which has been disaggregated for identified groups within the population. You must provide the results accurately and clearly. Sometimes you may want to include figures, graphs, or tables to visually present your results. These can be written as part of the narrative or they can be placed in the appendix. If they are in the appendix, let the reader know by a notation in the narrative.

Surveys, Questionnaires, Interviews

If you have used a survey, questionnaire, or interviews as the measure for data collection, you usually will have a large number of variables you could use for study. These variables emerge from the demographic data in the survey, questionnaire or interviews. You select the variables that are most specific to the purpose of the study. The variables selected should reflect those that are the most important and best illustrate the questions or issues you are investigating. Demographic variables may include age, length of service, assignment, education, gender, and ethnicity. These demographic variables can be used to disaggregate the data in terms of results. When reporting the results from the survey, questionnaire, or interview, write the statement exactly as it appears on the instrument. This statement is then followed by a report of the results in terms of each selected variable using the statistical measures you used to analyze responses to that variable. As the researcher, you may select some of the statements for detailed inclusion in the results. If you do so, you must provide a rationale for your choice of statements and provide a summary of the data from the remaining statements immediately following the analysis of the selected variables. If, in your survey or questionnaire you may have included a space for comments. You need to include pertinent comments in your study. These selected comments are listed immediately following your analysis of the data from the survey or questionnaire and the summary of the statements or questions not analyzed. Sometimes you may wish to have a space for comments after each statement on a survey or a question on a questionnaire. If this is so, the comments can be linked directly to the statement or question. Following your presentation of the results from selected variables, statements, and the summary of the results from the variables, you must prepare a summative statement about the results. This summative statement is designed to bring together the results in a brief way to review the totality of the results and to ensure that the reader has one more opportunity to review the study in terms of the all the results determined through your analyses. This summative statement does not have to be lengthy. If you have determined significance, be sure to report it. Include evidence of variance in terms of demographics and specific variables This summative statement should be brief, but with enough detail to ensure the reader clearly understands your results You will interpret the meaning of the results in the discussion section of the paper. If you have any questions about how to develop a survey or questionnaire see Appendix F, pages 137–140.

 ## Qualitative Results

First, the researcher needs to review the process of data collection as noted in the method section and to explain to the reader how the data was collected and analyzed. In qualitative studies you will be dealing with a large amount of data, much of it narrative data, collected through the various observations, interviews and other measures you used. In qualitative studies, you analyze these data. As researcher, you are responsible for the rich thick narrative that tells about both the formative and summative development of the study. Your narrative and findings should be comprehensive, expansive, and richly descriptive. You may need to code or categorize your data as the project develops. These codes or categories can develop and change as the study develops. Be sure to keep a detailed record of what has happened in the study on a daily or regular basis. The information you have gathered in the codes and categories can ensure that the detailed record of your study can be verified. As part of the narrative you may want to use figures or tables. You can do this as part of the narrative. You may also place figures and tables in an appendix. Be sure to follow APA guidelines for figures and tables. Through the process of analysis you have developed generalizations about the data. Your analyses and results have been gained throughout the qualitative process, but the results will be a synthesis of the generalizations in a descriptive narrative or an emerging theory grounded in the data you have collected. The mode of analysis in qualitative studies is inductive and is done by the researcher. From these generalizations, from the descriptive narrative, and from the emerging theory you have results that can provide meaning and substance for your colleagues. The descriptive narrative must be as complete as possible. Some deem it a richly descriptive narrative (Merriam, 1998). You are narrating the totality of the process involved in your study as well as the emerging information and grounded theory in this narrative. You inform the reader with clarity and a continuity the meaning of the study in terms of results which may include grounded theory. This is as far as you go in this section of your study. You write clearly, but include all the narrative and all the details necessary. Your narrative establishes the basis for conclusions and recommendations that are made in the discussion section of the paper. For further study you may wish to use descriptive, inferential or correlational statistical analyses with your data. Generalizability and application to similar populations are reserved for the discussion section of the paper.

Writing Tips

Again, when you are writing the results, you are dealing with technical terms as well as mathematical and statistical terms in quantitative studies. In qualitative studies you are dealing with narrative results and emerging theory. You may also be dealing with statistical data and analyses in qualitative studies if they need to be used. You need, however, to make these narrative results clear to the reader. In quantitative studies you must make sure that the reader does not get confused by the narrative, the terms, and the organization of the results. Results of the analysis of each variable should be discussed in simple terms within the narrative as well as in any figures or tables. The numbers need to be presented succinctly and clearly. Avoid simply presenting numbers and statistical data. If you are comparing results in variables make sure you clearly state what you are doing and why you are doing it. You may need to present the numbers, the data, and the comparisons in a figure or table so they can be seen and more easily understood by the reader. You may include the figures or tables in the text or place them in an appendix. Make sure your explanation of the results is organized and sequenced in a simple and logical order that makes sense to the reader. You may have to work on this explanation to make it readable and cogent for the reader. An introductory paragraph to the results section to inform the reader how you have organized the results including which statements or questions will be specifically analyzed and how you will organize the results section can be very helpful in orienting the reader to a clearer construct of the results section. Results must be understood to be used by your readers. Write your quantitative results in past or present perfect tense.

In qualitative studies you prepare a narrative of the results. The narrative is written in past tense or present perfect tense. An introductory paragraph on how you organized this section could be included, but may not be necessary. You must make sure that the reader understands how you developed your generalizations and how the theory emerged from the narrative. Great care must be taken in qualitative studies to ensure that the narrative has substance and meaning. You must make sure the findings and results are grounded in the data and that the inferences and emerging theory are logical and provide an evidentiary base. If you use figures or tables as part of your results, be sure to follow APA guidelines. In writing this narrative, the researcher must be sure that no bias, interpretation, or personal perspectives are apparent. Interpretations and personal perspectives are included only in the discussion section of your paper. In writing the results in both quantitative and qualitative studies, be sure that you have written with clarity, with cohesiveness, and in a cogent and careful manner. Use the past or present perfect tense in writing the results section of your study.

For a quick review of the elements necessary for inclusion in the results section refer to the checklist for the results section in Appendix A on page 116. The use of this checklist can help to ensure that you have included all components required in the results section for your study.

8 Preparing the Discussion

This is the final narrative section of your paper. It is titled discussion with that word centered one double space below the page header. In this *Handbook* the presentation of the discussion section of the paper is in two parts depending on whether you are writing a review of literature paper or a research study. For a review of literature paper there is a summary of the the literature reviewed and presented in the content of the review of literature. For a research study there is a summary of the review of literature, the method section, and the results section in the content of the discussion. Much of the content in both qualitative and quantitative studies is similar, but there are some differences. In both types of studies you follow the summary of the literature reviewed with your interpretation. Finally for both kinds of papers you would draw conclusions and develop recommendations based on the content of the review of literature and your interpretation. In research studies you compare and contrast the findings of your study with corollary studies in the review of literature and then develop your conclusions and your recommendations. In either type of paper, particularly for shorter papers or studies, you could write this section in narrative form without separating it into its component parts, though you may want to organize it into the component parts of summary, interpretation, conclusions, and recommendations. It is

It is important that you remember that this is your final narrative section of the paper and that it needs, like all the other sections, to be written clearly, carefully, and cogently.

important that you remember that this is your final narrative section of the paper and that it needs, like all the other sections, to be written clearly, carefully, and cogently.

Review of Literature Paper

In a review of literature paper you do these four things. First, you summarize the literature you have reviewed. Second, you interpret the literature reviewed. Third, you draw conclusions based on your interpretation and the content of the review, and fourth you make recommendations. This is the sequence of the discussion section in the review of literature papers. Follow this sequence. Do not change the order. Do not bring in any new resources, citations, or additional references in this section of the paper. Those were all done in the review of literature.

Summary

Your first task in the discussion is to summarize the literature you have reviewed for your paper. In a paragraph or a few paragraphs correlated with your categories summarize what you learned from the review of literature. This summary is a recap to help the reader in understanding the interpretation which comes next and to succinctly bring out the salient points of the review of literature. You will need to cite sources so the reader can better understand source of the information. The sources you cite should be your most important sources and should relate to the salient points you want to make in the interpretation. Remember that the sources you cite in the summary are the only ones you use for interpretation. You have cited the most important or salient resources and they are the ones you refer to in the interpretation section of the paper. You use the same sources for the interpretation. Do not add anything more to the summary. Do not cite new sources in the summary. The summary is written in the past tense or present perfect tense without comment. It is a succinct review of the most important things you found in the review of literature that pertain directly to the purpose of your paper.

Interpretation

This is the part of the discussion where you process your own interpretation and opinion about the literature you reviewed. Use only the sources noted in the summary. They are the sources you have deemed important and they are the sources you use to interpret the literature. Do not bring in new sources or make new citations.

In the interpretation you emphasize what you agree with and with what you disagree. You interpret, you compare and contrast, and you bridge the gaps. You give opinions and insights about the literature you reviewed. In the interpretation you provide the reader with your own perspective about the literature reviewed. This part of the discussion must be carefully constructed because your interpretations, insights, link-ages, and opinions provide the basis for your conclusions and recommendations. The evidence you have brought forward in your review of literature and that you have summarized in this discussion section provide, along with your interpretation, the evidentiary and logical rationale for your conclusions and for your recommendations.

Do not go into great detail. Keep the commentary focused on the literature noted in the summary and your interpretation of that literature. Do not be redundant. Your interpretation must be soundly based on what you have reported in the review of literature. You may write the interpretation in present tense. Think very carefully about what you want to say and how you have thought through the literature so you can write a logical and substantive interpretation that will be clear to the reader and provide the basis for your conclusions and recommendations. You need to ensure that the literature reviewed provided the evidentiary base for your conclusions and recommendations.

Conclusions

The conclusions you have drawn from your review of literature and your interpretation do not need to be lengthy. A sentence like "based on the review of literature and my interpretation of the literature, I have concluded that. . . ." is an appropriate open-ing sentence. Then you list your conclusions with no elaboration. The conclusions should be written in simple sentences and as briefly and efficiently as possible. You need only enough words to make your conclusion clear. You do not need to go into long or even brief explanations of the conclusions. Those were done in the interpre-tation section of the discussion. Your conclusions should stand alone as the summa-tive statements about what you have concluded and what the reader should also conclude. The rationale and evidentiary base for your conclusions were made appar-ent in the interpretation.

Recommendations

Recommendations are statements about what should be done, what should be implemented, or what changes should be made. These recommendations are based solely on your review of literature, your interpretations, and your conclusions. Recommendations, like the conclusions, should not be lengthy or complex. They should draw their evidentiary base from the literature, the interpretation and the conclusions. Recommendations should be written in the same manner as suggested above in the conclusions statement. Almost all papers need recommendations, only a few do not. For review of literature papers this is the final narrative statement of your paper. Do not go into an elaboration, or an explanation. Do not add any new mate-rial. State what you recommend as the last narrative statement of your paper. Succinctly stated and carefully written, recommendations can bring a strong closing to your paper.

For a quick review of the elements necessary for the discussion section of review of literature papers refer to the checklist in Appendix A on page 117. The use of this checklist will help ensure that you have included the required elements of the discussion section in your paper.

Research Studies

In the discussion section of a research study whether quantitative or qualitative, you follow the same structure and organization noted for review of literature papers. You summarize, next you interpret, then you draw conclusions, and finally you make recommendations. The organization is the same, but the content varies somewhat. Your obligation in the discussion of research studies is to summarize your findings and how they relate to the literature. You must ensure that your review of literature provided an evidentiary base for your conclusions and that the review included research studies related to your topic. If you have done this, you are ready to interpret the literature. In the interpretation you discuss the literature and research studies included in your summary. You also note your method, and your results. As you reviewed research studies related to your area of study you can interpret your method and results in terms of those studies. You then draw conclusions and make recommendations on the basis of the literature, the method, and of the results of your study. This chapter or section of your paper is of great importance because you are presenting a professional discussion of what you learned, how you interpreted it, and what you concluded and recommended. This is the final and summative statement of what you have done. You have completed a research study that has importance in your field and you need to disseminate it clearly with emphasis on what the research study means to you and to your colleagues in the profession.

Summary

In this summary component of results you do two things. You summarize the review of literature and you summarize your findings. In the review of literature you focused on the works of researchers, the outcomes of studies, and important sources in your particular area of study. You have prepared the review of literature in terms of the purpose of your study and here you summarize the salient points of that review in terms of the focus and purpose of the study. You then summarize your method and your results in terms of the studies you have reviewed. Your summary of results is a summative statement and should include your most pertinent findings.

Once you have stated your results you need to summarize the literature related to your study. Make sure you have included a summary of studies related to your purpose including their methods and findings. You should focus only the major sources and research studies closely related to your study. You will need to include citations so readers know your major sources. Do not bring in any new sources here, you are simply summarizing your findings and the review of literature. Make sure that what you write in the summary are the salient points within the literature you have reviewed. Remember not to interpret nor elaborate on any findings nor any literature in this section of results. Simply tell what you found and identify and summarize the literature closely related to your study. This summary of literature reviewed should be used in conjunction with the results from your study. The summary should be written in the past tense or present perfect tense.

Interpretation

Here you present your own views on what you have done and what your results mean both in terms of your study and in terms of related literature and other studies in the field. Note how your study related to, correlated with, or was different from other studies in the field. Show where and how you method and findings agreed were similar to or different from other studies. You compare and contrast, you interpret similarities and differences, and you bridge the gaps. You may include in your narrative figures, tables, and graphs as needed to visually show your results. These would be figures, tables, and graphs already introduced in the results section. From your study do not include new tables, figures or graphs. You can also include figures, tables, and graphs from prior studies specific to your study if they have been included in the review of literature or in the summary. For your interpretation comment only on the sources, tables, figures or graphs you have referred to in the summary. It is only then they can be introduced in this section of the study. These figures, tables, and graphs could also be placed in an appendix.

Discuss any theories or ideas that you have confirmed. Interpret your findings in terms of their consistency or not consistency with other studies. You compare and contrast your findings with other research in the field and interpret similarities and differences. You must identify significance or lack of significance in terms of the variables tested in quantitative studies if you are using inferential statistical measures. If you are using correlational statistical measures you need to show how identified variables correlate or do not correlate with each other. You must point out in qualitative studies your generalizations and any grounded theory that emerged from the study. You need to emphasize how your results relate to other studies and to the literature you have reviewed in your field of study. The interpretation component of the discussion is extremely important. You write it with care and concern because the successful dissemination of your findings will be based largely on this section of the paper. The generalizability of your results for other similar populations will be based on this interpretation of your study.

As you write the interpretation, readers need to clearly understand what you have found and how your findings relate to the area of study. You emphasize in your closing paragraphs what you feel are the most important findings and the points that highlight what you consider to be important for your colleagues in the field. Be as direct as you need and emphasize the importance of those findings. The final paragraphs of your interpretation should contain the summative statement of your findings, their importance, and how they relate to the area of study. It is from these culminating evidentiary statements in the interpretation that you draw your conclusions and your recommendations.

Conclusions

Your conclusions are drawn directly from the review of literature and the interpretation of the literature, the method, and the results. They should be linked to the summative statements in your interpretation. Conclusions should be written clearly and with the use of only the words needed to state what you have concluded. Conclusions are not lengthy, nor are they convoluted. They are concise and straight forward statements. Conclusions should reflect what you found and carry the conclusive message of your paper. A sentence beginning "based on the review of literature and the findings of this study I have concluded that. . . ." This is all that is needed. Do not elaborate or explain. That was done in the interpretation. Both quantitative and qualitative studies follow this pattern. In qualitative studies you should note any grounded theory emerging from your study. Nothing further needs to be written.

Recommendations

Your recommendations are based on your results, your review of literature, your interpretation, and your conclusions. A recommendation is your statement about what you feel needs yet to be done, on generalizability to specific groups, on implementation and use, or on further research that should be done in the area of the study. You are making your last narrative statement of the study and your conclusions and recommendations are the final comments you make. Recommendations should be cast in clear, concise, and confident language and attest to a job well done. You do not need to explain the recommendations or elaborate on them. They are your final succinct statements of a study done with care and attention to the process and to the outcomes. Recommendations are what you project for future studies or for implementation of results.

For a quick review of the expected elements of the discussion section of a research study refer to the checklist in Appendix A on page 118. The use of this checklist will help ensure that you have included all the required components of this section of your research study.

Writing Tips

These writing tips apply to both review of literature papers and to research studies except where noted. The discussion section of the paper or study can be written as a narrative without categories and subcategories or you can organize it with categories. If your paper is relatively brief, do not organize this section into categories. If you use categories you can name them summary, interpretation, conclusions, and recommendations. Subcategories in a research study could be the names of the categories of your method section such as population, variables, analyses and so forth. If you choose to have categories and subcategories you will need to follow APA guidelines. In almost every case, however, you will not use subcategories.

In this final section of the paper or study you will continue to use citations to keep the reader informed about the sources to which you are referring. Citations are necessary only in the summary and interpretation components of the discussion. They should not be used for conclusions or recommendations Do not introduce any new sources in the discussion. Be sure to use the APA style and format for all citations. All of your citations should refer to sources within the review of literature. For the interpretation section remember that you use only the information and sources provided in the summary. In the interpretation section you point out what was most important in the literature as it relates to your interpretation.

In a research study you also need to identify your findings and interpret them as they relate to the literature you reviewed. In both quantitative and qualitative studies you express your own opinion only in the interpretation category of the discussion section. Express your personal opinions along with your conclusions and recommendations. This chapter or section is the only place in the paper or study where you present personal opinions and interpretations. This is where you can be emphatic and confident. This is where you make the final determination about the importance and worth of your paper or your study. Make sure that the final paragraphs in the interpretation clearly state what you consider to be most important to the reader. This becomes the link to your conclusions and your recommendations.

While some of the writing in this section is in the past tense or present perfect tense, in particular the summary, you can present your interpretations, opinions, conclusions, and recommendations in the present tense. Your recommendations can, in some instances, be in the future tense. In the discussion you present your summary and findings. You also tell the reader how you interpreted the literature and the findings. In terms of your findings you both interpret them and suggest meanings. Be sure that the meaning of the study is consistent with the results. In the interpretation you will also need to compare and contrast your findings with related studies you reviewed. The review of literature should provide an integral part of the evidentiary base for your study. This is also where you present your opinions. In the discussion you compare and contrast, bridge the gaps, judge and interpret. Here is where you conclude and where you recommend. Indeed, this is what the discussion is all about.

In the interpretation component of the discussion you can use the personal pronoun I or if there is more than one author the personal pronoun we. It is wise, however, to minimize the use of I or we. Let what has been written speak for itself. Do not, however, refer to yourself as the author. You can also write in the present tense except in the summary. When you make recommendations you may, if appropriate, use the future tense. You have the opportunity, in this section, to reflect you personal perspectives and opinions. You will strongly support your professional findings and positions in terms of the interpretation, conclusions, and recommendations as long as they are supported by evidence from the review of literature and from the results. This is where you react to the issues, problems, and questions inherent within the paper. You do this based on the review of literature and the findings if you did a research paper. You do not bring in any new resources. What you have done needs to rest on its own integrity. You present your paper from your own professional perspective.

When you have completed this section of the paper you have finished a well organized and properly sequenced professional paper. Be sure to edit it and refine the rough drafts. One good way to do this is to read it aloud. You can quickly hear problems of organization, continuity, and syntax, and make the necessary corrections. Another good way to edit the paper is to have a peer or someone else critique it. Be sure to find someone who will be objective and provide positive suggestions and ideas for you in terms of editing your paper. Once the final editing is done, you will have completed the professional preparation of your paper. It will be ready for a professional reader to review it and ready for publication.

In writing your paper, do not procrastinate. Start as soon as you have defined the topic. Define the topic as quickly as possible. You know that you have a deadline to meet, so follow a schedule. Sometimes the schedule may be set by the instructor. Sometimes you need to develop a personal timeline for completion of the paper or study. Above all, do not wait until late in the class time frame or the report schedule to start your paper. In some instances the instructor or supervisor may be willing to review your paper or consult with you if you have any problems. Take advantage of those reviews and consultations. If your instructor or supervisor will review the paper, turn in a rough draft or what you have completed at the time designated by the instructor or supervisor. The review by the instructor or supervisor as well as consultations with others can help you produce a much better paper, perhaps one that will be published in some context.

Just a word about plagiarism. Remember that you can use direct quotes, you can paraphrase, and you summarize a writer's work. You must, however, always cite the source. Using an author's words directly without citation constitutes plagiarism and will result in a seriously marred paper or a failing grade. Your reader will check for plagiarism. Start gathering resources in an organized manner. Note all the bibliographical information for any source reviewed and cited in your paper. Annotate pertinent resources. Also write down appropriate quotes and key them to page numbers. Cite them in your paper. Once you have identified the categories, put your sources along with quotes and bibliographical information in categories or on colored cards so they are keyed to your categories. Develop a personal system for organizing and categorizing information. In writing your paper, set a time line and keep to it. Build into the time line checkpoints and benchmarks for completing certain sections and for editing purposes. Formal papers take consistent and careful effort and time. Be sure that you put in as much time as you will need. Keep this *Handbook* close by for reference and as a resource for writing your paper. Best wishes to you in your writing process and congratulations on finishing this last narrative section of your paper. For a quick review of the discussion section see checklists pages 117 and 118.

9   Preparing the References

The final section of your paper is the reference section. This section is titled references. It is not a part of the narrative, but it is an integral and essential section of your paper and is numbered as part of the paper with a page header. In this section you include only the references you have cited in the paper. Do not include any other references. This is not a bibliography. It is a list of sources you have referred to in your paper. Be sure that every entry and every line in the reference section is double spaced. Your reader will check the citations and references carefully and match them with each other. Your reader will also check to ensure that you have followed the format of the APA. It is, therefore, essential that you follow the APA format. You will find clear and specific formats for all kinds of references in the *Publication Manual of the American Psychological Association.* A list of the most common references is also provided for you in the Appendix E beginning on page 137 of this handbook. It should be noted here that personal communications are not included in the reference section. See page 53 for a discussion of how to format them.

Personal communications are included only in the narrative sections of the paper, not in the reference section. You must ensure that all references are alphabetized by author. If no author is listed for the source, the title of the source is used. If there is no title a concise descriptor of the source is used. Again, all references are listed in alphabetic sequence including those

> *In this section you include only the references you have cited in the paper. Do not include any other references. This is not a bibliography.*

without an author named. The reference format is called a hanging reference. This means that the first line of each reference is justified to the left margin. Succeeding lines in the reference are tabbed with the same number of spaces you used for the tabbing of your paper. If you are referencing an internet source, include the pathway and be sure the pathway is not underlined and that it is always written in black with an APA approved typeface. Times New Roman, Arial, or similar are approved APA typefaces. Do not put a period after the pathway unless it is a part of it. You must also include the date you downloaded or reviewed the internet source. The references for this work are found on page 105. This is an example of how your reference section should be organized and formatted.

Writing Tips

For a quick review of the elements of the reference section, please refer to the checklist for references found in Appendix A on page 119. The use of this checklist will help ensure that you have completed the required components of the reference section.

10 Bibliography and Appendixes

It should be noted here that you may include a bibliography and appendixes in your paper. These are not essential elements of the paper, but you may want to include them if you feel they are needed. A bibliography is a list of resources not in the references, but which pertain to the topic or the study. Do not include sources that do not correlate with your topic or to your study. The bibliography is not a part of your narrative paper, nor is it a part of the reference section. If you include a bibliography as additional source material, it is a good idea to do a brief annotation of each resource so the reader can select material of interest that will provide for supplemental personal reading in the field. The annotation is blocked and begins one double space below the entry. It is not indented. The bibliography immediately follows the reference section of your paper. A bibliography has a page header for each page and is sequenced with the paper or the study.

Appendixes, if you have included them, are placed following the reference section of your paper and the bibliography if one is included. When there is more than one appendix, they are usually lettered A, B, C, D and so forth. If the paper has only one appendix, it is simply referred to as the appendix. Each appendix must have a title. Appendixes may include tables, figures, statistical information, illustrations or narrative, and any additional supplemental material you feel is important for reader information. In the body of the paper, usually in the

> A bibliography is a list of resources not in the references, but which pertain to the topic or the study.

method, the results, or in the discussion sections, you can refer to the appendix pertinent to the information or to the interpretation presented. Be sure to follow APA style and format for all appendixes.

For a quick review of the elements of the bibliography see the checklist for bibliography in Appendix A page 122. For a review of the elements of appendixes refer to the checklist for appendixes in Appendix A page 121. The use of these checklists will help ensure that you have completed the required components of the bibliography and the appendix in the correct format.

11 Common Problems in Writing Formal Papers

Chapter

Over the years we have read thousands of formal papers. We are, here, focusing on some of the more common errors, problems, and issues we have found in student writing. The *Publication Manual of the American Psychological Association* provides an excellent source for helping you in the writing process. The information in this *Handbook* is consistent with that manual. There are other fine manuals and resources available to you as well, some of which we have already cited. What we have done here, however, is to provide a compendium of common problems, issues, and errors in graduate and formal papers we have read over the past years. They are listed in alphabetic order. We consistently find these problems, isssues, and errors in papers. Be cognizant of them as you write your own paper.

Abstract

The abstract is noted as page two of your paper. It consists of from 120 to 150 words and includes the purpose of the paper or study and salient points you have found. Major findings, if you have written a research study, are included. Conclusions and recommendations should also be included. The abstract is not indented; it is blocked.

Agreement

Referents should agree in gender and number. This statement encapsulates the

An ellipsis is used when you leave a word or words out of a direct quote for clarity of meaning.

nature of these kinds of errors. Verbs and pronouns should agree in gender and number with the subject. In this era of politically correct writing, we have frequently read papers where the author has used a single subject such as student and has then used they, their, or them rather than having noun pronoun agreement. This is not acceptable in formal papers. You can use he/she if you wish, but avoid this as much as possible. In most instances you can, through careful writing, avoid the heeshees and remain consistent in terms of subject pronoun agreement. There should also be agreement in gender and number with subject and verb. Review your paper carefully to correct any such errors.

Among *and* Between

You should note that when you are comparing and contrasting or making a statement discussing difference between pairs and groups you use *among* when referring to more than two or more than groups of two. You use *between* when referring only to groups of two or to pairs of groups.

Anthropomorphisms

An anthropomorphism occurs when ascribing human characteristics to animals or inanimate objects. Remember that research cannot say, infer, demonstrate, show, or indicate. Only researchers, writers, or authors can write, infer, demonstrate, show, or indicate. This is a very common error by writers of formal papers including some which occur in published papers and books. Avoid anthropomorphisms. They indicate sloppiness of style and careless construction.

Author Reference

Use the personal pronoun I with great care throughout the paper. Do not use the third person or refer to yourself as the author of the paper. Whenever you need to refer to yourself use the personal pronoun I. If the paper has two or more authors use we. Minimize the use of I throughout the paper. Use it when you note why I chose the paper in the introduction and when you interpret, conclude, and recommend in the discussion section. It is seldom, if ever, used in other sections of the paper.

Categories

The categories represent the major parts of any narrative section of your paper. They are most frequently used in the review of literature, but can be used in other sections of your paper or study as needed. Categories are generally used in the method section of a research study and in the results section. Other than in the review of literature, if your paper is relatively brief, you may not need to use them. The name of the category is written in italics and is on a separate line in the narrative. All words except articles and prepositions are capitalized. Keep the names of the categories as brief as possible. You must have at least two categories in any section of the paper to justify their use.

 ## Citations

Citations are simple to do, but if in doubt refer to the APA *Manual*. The usual citation is the author's last name followed by a comma and the year of publication. If no date of publication is given use the initials n.d. in lower case. This information is in parentheses. You may use the author's name as part of a sentence. If you do, follow it with the year of publication in parentheses. When a work has no author use the first two words of the title. If there is no author or title use a brief descriptor of the content not to exceed two words. These are the first two words of your reference. If you are using a direct quote, you must use the author's name, the year, and the page number of the quotation. Direct quotes of less than forty words require quotation marks. Direct quotes of forty or more words are blocked without the use of quotation marks. If the quote is from a short internet article use the abbreviation para. followed by the paragraph number. You may also use the paragraph symbol. Check the most recent edition of the APA *Manual* for additional information on electronic citations and references.

Colloquialisms

Avoid the use of colloquial language. In a formal paper, this is unacceptable except in rare circumstances or unless the colloquialism occurs in a direct quote. A colloquialism is informal or idiomatic speech or writing and should not be used in formal papers. The most common colloquialism we have seen in papers is "a lot" meaning many or frequent. Writers forget that a lot is a small area of ground on which structures can be built. Avoid also the use of idioms and slang expressions.

Ellipses

An ellipsis is used when you leave a word or words out of a direct quote for clarity of meaning. An ellipsis is shown by three dots to signify that a word or words have been omitted from the quote. You make an ellipsis by doing a dot with a space between dots three times to show words omitted. Use four dots with a space between each dot when the omitted words occur in two or more sentences. Generally do not begin or end a quote with ellipses.

Hyphens

Do not end a line or begin a line of the narrative with a hyphen. Use hyphens as defined by the APA. Self, when it is linked to a characteristic is always hyphenated. Non does not need a hyphen. It can stand alone or be linked to its characteristic such as *nondirective*.

If *as Conditional*

When writing in the past tense always use were when following the noun or pronoun with a past tense form of to be. If, in this sense, is a conditional and requires the use of were.

Justification

The paper is justified only on the left margin. Do not justify on the right margin of the paper. All lines of citations of forty or more words are justified one tab space from the left margin. The right margin in citations is not justified with one exception. Only the page header and the numbers of the pages in the table of contents are justified on the right margin. Block quotations are justified one tab space from the left margin in all lines. Quotation marks are not used to open or close a block quote. If a quotation is included in a blocked quote use only one quotation mark (') at the beginning and end of the quote.

Language

Use specific and precise language. Eliminate redundancies. Do not use slang expressions or colloquialisms. Check your choice of words and make sure that you are saying what you want to say with an economy of expression. Say only what needs to be said. Avoid jargon or the continual use of technical language. While some technical or professional terminology may be necessary, the continual use of such language can be distracting and irritating to the reader. Presentation of ideas must be orderly and sequential. Use punctuation to provide clarity and continuity. Use transitional words and pronouns to provide for additional clarity and continuity. Use simple sentences most of the time. Use compound or complex sentences only when necessary.

Numbers

Numbers zero through nine must be written out. Numbers ten and over can be written in their Arabic form. Numbers are always written out at the beginning of a sentences such as: Seventy-four percent.

Quotations

There is an expectation that you use direct quotes in your paper. If the quote is less than 40 words it is included in the narrative with quotation marks at the beginning of the quote and at the end of the quote. All quotations must have a citation with a page or paragraph number. For quotations of 40 or more words, each line of the quotation is blocked one tab space from the left margin. If there is a quotation within the quotation us a single quotation mark (') at the beginning and end of the quote within the quotation.

Personal Communications

These refer to people consulted or interviewed during the preparation of your paper. Personal communications can also be memos, e-mails, and other electronic resources. You may quote or paraphrase the information you have gained from them in the narrative sections of your paper. Most frequently these occur in the review of literature. If the personal communication is used for a direct quote follow the format for quotations. Use initials and surname in the citation. Personal communications are cited as follows: J. Doe, (personal communication, June 21, 2005) or (J. W. Doe, personal communication, June 21, 2005) They are cited in the text only and are not included in the reference section.

Plagiarism

Plagiarism means to copy someone's work and claiming it as your own. You must provide a citation for every statement in your paper except the selection of the topic, why you chose the topic, in the interpretion component of the discussion, and in the conclusions, and recommendations. For every other part of the paper you must give credit to the source. Your reader will check for plagiarism. If you have plagiarized content in any part of your paper it will result in a failing grade or a rejection of your paper.

Redundancy

While redundancy may sometimes be used in the discussion section to be emphatic, it should be avoided throughout your paper. Your paper is stronger without it. Do not be emphatic through redundancy. If you wish to emphasize a point in the discussion section, let the reader know that you feel it is important. It may sometimes be necessary to restate an idea, thought, or interpretation for clarity and emphasis, but do it in language different than the original so that it becomes a logical followup to what you have already written.

Referents

Be very careful about referents. Be sure the reader clearly understands what you are referring to when you use a pronoun to refer to the subject. Referent problems occur most often when you are citing an author and continue discussing the work. Include a restatement of the author's name or the subject of the discussion no later than three to six sentences from the first referent. Referents should agree in gender and number. Do not use we or our to refer to groups of people in your profession. Always use the name of the group of people to whom you are referring.

Spacing

Just a simple reminder. Everything in your paper is double spaced. The use of any other spacing constitutes a format error. The reference section and direct quotes of more than 40 words are double spaced along with every other section of your paper. Text begins one double space below the page header. Improper spacing, as has been noted, is a format error.

Subcategories

The use of subcategories may be necessary, particularly in the review of literature, when you have a category that needs to have more than one area of focus. For example, if you are doing a paper in which one of your categories is instructional strategies, you may have subcategories on each of the specific strategies about which you have reviewed literature. A subcategory is indented one tab space from the left margin. It is written in italics and is followed by a period. The text begins immediately following the notation of the subcategory.

Superscript and Subscript

Do not use superscript or subscript except in mathematical or scientific formulae or as approved by the APA. Do not use superscript in the reference section when referring to the edition of a book.

Syntax

Sentence structure is important. Write clearly, sequentially, and logically. Use simple sentences for the most part. Say only what needs to be said. Compound and complex sentences should be used only when needed and to clarify the information presented. Comma splices (sometimes called comma faults), run on sentences, and fragments are major syntax errors and could seriously affect the quality of your paper and your grade. Major syntax errors would certainly be noted by an editor or publisher. Fragments occur most frequently when you begin a sentence with an adverb. Be sure to review your paper for syntax errors.

 Tense

This is one of the most common errors we have seen in papers. In formal papers you use the past tense or the present perfect tense consistently in the abstract, introduction, and review of literature. You also use the past or present perfect tense in the method and results sections of a research study. The present perfect tense refers to an action that did not occur at a specific defined time or occurred in the past and is continuing. Remember that when the reader reviews your paper you have already completed the paper. All literature or research you cite in your paper has been completed. The only exception for the use of the past or present perfect tense is within direct quotes when the writer you are quoting uses a tense other than the past tense or present perfect tense. In the discussion section of your paper you use the past tense or present perfect tense in the summary or when referring to the literature reviewed. You may use the present tense, the future tense, or other tenses in the discussion section of your paper or study when you are interpreting, comparing and contrasting, expressing your professional opinions, drawing conclusions or making recommendations.

 That *and* Who

Use who or whom to refer to humans. Use that or which to refer to animals. This is a frequent error and needs to be avoided.

 Typeface

Use only typefaces approved by the APA. You must use 12 point size only. APA recommends Times New Roman, Courier, or similar. No superscript or subscript may be used except in specified scientific or mathematics symbols or formulae. Do not use superscript in the reference section. Eliminate any color other than black in the reference section including internet pathways.

Voice

Use the active voice rather than the passive voice in your writing in most instances. The active voice is a direct communicator of ideas and meaning and the active voice fits well into the context of formal papers. The passive voice is used only when you want to focus on the object of the action or the recipient of the action. Proper use of voice makes for clearer communication of the content of your paper.

12 Formal Writing Conventions

Formal writing is a style used by those who are preparing papers, reviews of literature, research studies, and formal documents for a specific audience. As noted in the preface, formal writing is a pristine exercise in clarity, continuity, and cogent thinking. Following the conventions of formal writing helps ensure that this occurs in papers, documents, and research studies. Formal writing is consistently used when writing a review of literature paper or a research study. Formal writing is used for some reports, for monographs, and for a variety of other formal documents. Formal writing can also be used for preparing narrative journal articles or formal reports to designated groups. Formal writing is a style that can be easily learned. It does, however, have certain conventions which need to be followed and used in the preparation of the document you plan to submit. Listed below are some of the conventions of formal writing.

Organization

Formal writing is organized into sections or chapters according to the length of the paper. Generally in papers under fifty pages one does not use chapters. Use section headings. For longer papers, monographs, or narrative documents chapters may be used as headings with the title of the chapter centered one double space below the number of the chapter which is written in upper case Roman numerals. When writing a review

> Formal writing is a pristine exercise in clarity, continuity, and cogent thinking.

of literature paper, three sections will be used. They are introduction, review of literature, and discussion. The full title of the paper is used in the introduction. The next sections are entitled review of literature and discussion. For research studies there are five sections. They are introduction, review of literature, method, results, and discussion. The full title is used in the introduction. The succeeding sections are entitled as review of literature, method, results, and discussion. For theses or dissertations of more than fifty pages, these five sections can be noted as chapters. In writing formal papers for journals, these sections may not be necessary. For formal reports and documents, follow a narrative sequence or any structure set by the organization to which the document or formal report is to be submitted. This may entail identifying sections by specific names needed for the audience. An abstract of from 120–150 words follows the title page and precedes content. A table of contents may be expected, particularly in research studies, monographs, and in some formal reports or documents.

Syntax

Formal writing should be strait forward, strong and cogent. Formal writing should be easily understood by the readers. You are generally writing for audiences familiar with the area of the study or for audiences who want to learn more about the topic or study. Syntax is very important. Most of the time use short simple sentences. Use complex or compound sentences only when necessary. Usually over eighty percent of the sentences should be simple sentences. Use technical language only when needed. The well wrought paper will flow effectively if sentences are clearly understood by the reader. Avoid syntactical usage that would result in choppiness and reduce the cogency of the paper. This sometimes happens if only simple sentences are over used. Compound and complex sentences can be used occasionally to make the flow of the paper smoother and more efficient. Do not add extra wording to sentences or try to impress the reader with your erudition. Remember that verbosity is the last refuge of mediocrity. Say only what needs to be said and say it mostly in short, clear, and carefully wrought simple sentences. The appropriate use of syntax can greatly enhance your paper.

Related to syntax is the structure of paragraphs. Paragraphs should not be lengthy. Four to fifteen lines should encompass the length of a paragraph. Paragraphs are organized around a specific topic. Often the topic is stated in the initial sentence, but it can be noted later in the paragraph. The meaning of the paragraph may, however, become apparent only through the whole narrative of the paragraph. The effective use of paragraphs can strengthen the paper and provide for fluent structure, clarity, and sequence for readers.

Word Usage

The selection of the right word is very important in formal writing. Use the precise word in each sentence for clarity of meaning. Word usage in an appropriate syntactical structure can ensure continuity and cogency. Keep a dictionary and a thesaurus close by for reference when writing a formal paper. The right words in the right place are strong virtues in formal writing. It is necessary that you avoid colloquialisms, idiomatic expressions, and slang. You are writing a formal paper and the use of those kinds of words or phrases can deter from meaning, bring about an uncomfortable response from the reader, and can reduce the the sequence and flow of the paper. Avoid the use of too many descriptors for nouns. When several descriptors are used, break them out into individual sentences.

It is also very important to avoid value oriented words throughout the paper with the exception of portions of the discussion when interpreting, drawing conclusions, or making recommendations. Even in those portions of the discussion they should be used sparingly, if at all. The use of value oriented words earlier can, and usually do, show your biases and your opinions. These have no place in a formal paper except in the interpretation, conclusions, and recommendations. You are not writing a polemic. You are writing a formal paper that should be as objective as possible until you interpret, analyze, conclude, and recommend. These interpretations, analyses, conclusions, and recommendations are based on your objective review of literature and on the methods and results you have found if you are writing a research study. As you review your paper, look also for words that are not precise or which can be interpreted in more than one way. Change, whenever possible, any word that could be interpreted in more than one way. Make changes for precision of language and for the continuity and cogency of the paper. The proper use of words is essential in any formal paper.

Tense

The tenses of choice in formal writing are past and present perfect. The past tense is used consistently throughout the paper for citations and references to the sources you have used. The past tense or present perfect tense are used in every section of the paper with the exception that you may use the present tense or the future tense in the interpretation, conclusion, and recommendation components of the discussion section. The only other exception occurs when a direct quote is used in the paper and contains a tense other than past or present perfect. Present perfect tense is used for an event or issue that started in the past and has been continuing. In the body of the paper the use of past or present perfect is consistent until the discussion section of the paper. In that section the present tense can be used, as noted above, for the interpretation, the conclusions, and the recommendations. When writing the recommendations the future tense may be used. The rationale for using the past tense or present perfect tense is that every source cited or reference has already been written. Even citations from the internet have been posted before you read the paper. A further rationale is that your readers will have read your paper as something that was done in the past and that they are reading from that perspective. This may be one of the conventions that may be the most difficult to accommodate because writers are conditioned to write in the present tense or other tenses. It is important, however that you adhere strictly to this convention when writing formal papers.

Quotations and Paraphrases

Every statement of information in a formal paper with a few exceptions must be based upon the ideas and writings of the authors of your sources. The exceptions in the body of the paper are in the purpose statement and the rationale for selecting topic. Additional exceptions are in the interpretation, conclusions, and recommendations. No opinions, personal perspectives, or added comment can be made in any other section of a formal paper. Every new fact, idea, information, or point of view must come from a source and be cited. Direct quotes from the source may be used. Paraphrases may also be used. They must be cited. Each quotation or paragraph must have a citation. Direct quotes of less than forty words are shown by quotation marks at the beginning of the quotation and at the end of the quotation. This is followed by the author, the date, and the page number from the source. Quotations of forty or more words are blocked and do not have quotation marks around them Blocked quotes are followed by a citation of the author, year of publication, and page number. You may use paraphrases from a source. These paraphrases must be documented by a citation. Paraphrases are used when you summarizing an author's ideas, narrative, or perspective. Do not add any personal comments or reaction to the paraphrase. You do that in the interpretation component of the discussion section. Your reader will almost always check your sources and will be aware of any personal comments you may have added. It is very important to remember this when writing a formal paper.

References and Bibliography

References and bibliographies are two different elements of a formal paper. References are a compilation of the sources you have cited in the paper. They are listed alphabetically by last name of author. Use only initials for first and middle name. A reference section is required for formal papers in which citations have been made. You need to follow the style manual your university, organization, or corporation recommends. We are using the format provided by the American Psychological Association in their latest publication manual in this *Handbook*. Be sure that you follow the structure of the format for each reference. There are more than a hundred variations and you must select the one that needs to be used for every specific reference. When making citations and preparing for their inclusion in the reference section of the paper, be sure you have all the correct bibliographical information. Many readers will refer to the reference section when citations are made in the body of the work.

Bibliographies are not necessarily a part of a formal paper. They can, however be included as a separate section following the reference section. A bibliography is an alphabetized list of sources pertinent to the area of study, but not included in the reference section. Do not include any of the sources listed in the reference section of the paper or study. Make sure that the sources listed in the bibliography pertain to the topic of the paper. To ensure that the reader understands this, a brief annotation for each work in the bibliography can be included. We recommend a brief annotation for each listing in the bibliography. Annotations can be brief, but must reflect a relationship to the topic. Bibliographies without annotations can be included, but have little use for the reader. The purpose of the bibliography is to provide the reader with additional sources for further reading and study. We, therefore, strongly recommend an annotated bibliography.

Other Formal Writing Conventions

There are a number of other conventions. Among these are the elimination of anthropomorphisms, the use of the active voice, avoiding redundancies, appropriate use of ellipses, the use of the correct typefaces and font size, the proper use of that and who, among and between, and references to the author. All these and others are discussed in the *Handbook*. Please refer to the section of the *Handbook* that pertains to any questions about these and other formal writing conventions. In the *Handbook* you will not only find information about the writing conventions mentioned above, but useful tips on organization, writing, sequence, and structure. Explanations of many of these conventions are found in the Common Errors section of the *Handbook*. Please also refer to the grammar section for additional guidelines and assistance in writing. The grammar section of this *Handbook* can also be of help to you. Be sure to check the index for specific help. Information is keyed to the page or pages of the *Handbook and* where it can be found through the index.

Additional Applications

Formal writing conventions are used in many other contexts. If you are in education and are working on policy or are on a committee working on curriculum, instruction, evaluation, policy, or any other issue, formal writing conventions need to be used for any papers to be presented or reports to be prepared. Narrative reports of action research done within the classroom or the school also need to be written using formal writing conventions. In education, business or other professions, formal writing conventions must be used for white papers, reports, committee summaries, monographs, theses, dissertations, and other formal instruments. The use of formal writing conventions can be applied in any context where there is a need for a clear, concise, and well wrought document. In any of these contexts the use of formal writing conventions can be a responsive and lucid organizational structure available to meet the needs of the writers for their presentations. We encourage the use of these conventions in any professional exercise involving, study, analysis, synthesis, and evaluation. Formal writing conventions can meet the needs of people in any profession and in any circumstance where reporting is needed.

Summary

What we have done in this section of the *Handbook* is to cluster together some of the major conventions of formal writing as well as to briefly refer to others. In some cases this is redundant to what was presented earlier in the *Handbook*. We felt, however, that this reiteration was necessary and positive and would provide a quick overview of formal writing conventions as well as an additional perspective on protocols that must be followed in formal papers. This focus on formal writing conventions provides yet another perspective on developing your formal paper, report, or document. We have provided a brief insight into a number of the conventions of formal writing. It can serve as a strong and useful adjunct to the *Handbook*. Our best wishes to you as you work on and complete your formal papers utilizing the *Handbook* and this summary of formal writing conventions.

Writing Tips

For a quick review of these conventions, refer to the checklist on conventions of formal writing found in Appendix A page 120. The use of the checklist will provide a further review of your paper in terms of formal writing.

13 Preparing Formal Reports or White Papers

In preparing formal reports, also called white papers, the conventions of formal writing are followed consistently. Formal reports or white papers are specific to identified audiences. It is imperative that any parameters or expectations concerning the audience for which you are writing are specifically followed. Your purpose in a formal report is to explore an issue or problem, examine the elements within the problem, review literature pertinent to the problem or issue, discuss them, and develop conclusions and recommendations that could provide information about the problem or issue and which could resolve or ameliorate the problem or issue. The formal report or white paper has four parts. They are introduction, background, current practices, and conclusions and recommendations. Your report will also include citations of literature reviewed, any personal communications, and references.

Introduction

In the introduction you will first state the purpose of the report or white paper clearly and concisely. You will also establish the importance of the report or white paper by providing general information about the topic, problem, or issue. In the importance of the report or white paper you will need to cite sources from literature

> The formal report or white paper has four parts. They are introduction, background, current practices, and conclusions and recommendations.

pertinent to the problem. You may use personal communications with those involved in the issue and cite those personal communications. Personal communications are listed in the narrative of the paper, but not in the reference section. Through these citations and personal communications, you establish the importance of the report. Further, you need to provide a brief review of the existing situation.

Your introduction should be relatively short and should inform your audience clearly and concisely your purpose, your definition of the problem or issue, and why the report or white paper is important to the audience. Through identifying the importance of the report or white paper, you establish the need for the report or white paper. You further show why it is important to the audience. After you have defined the problem you will present information on the existing situation and the current status of the issue or problem. In the introduction all these pertinent factors and the current status of the problem or issue are succinctly presented, resources are cited to establish both the need for the report or white paper and to clearly define the issue or problem presented from information and interviews with people involved in the problem as well as literature about similar issues and problem. Through the introduction, the stage is set for the next section of the white paper or formal report. That section is the background.

Background

In the background section of your formal report or white paper you provide information specific to your company, your community, your school, or your school district. You review how the issue or problem has been being addressed by personnel assigned to it or those responsible for oversight. You review current processes, practices, and interventions already in place in the context of the problem being reviewed. Further, you review the history of the problem. You explore how the problem or the issue has been addressed earlier and what changes have taken place since the problem was initially found to be an issue. You will also show how it is affecting or impacting personnel, residents, teachers, parents, management, and administrators. It is your obligation in formal reports or white papers to include all this background information as well as the history of the problem.

You will, in addition, include information on how other companies, schools, or school districts have dealt with the issue or similar problems. To gather this information you may need to interact with participants, review historical documents, conduct interviews, and cite related literature. Material in the background section should focus only the problem or issue you are reviewing and discussing. It should not be too broad in its scope. Include citations and personal communications as part of the background information. In this section of your formal report or white paper it is essential for the audience to gain a perspective on how you have defined the issues and problems in context and how they have been addressed historically. The audience should also be informed about how the issue or problem and the history of how this problem or issue has been handled by other similar companies, schools, or school districts. It is important that this section of your paper be clearly, concisely, and cogently written.

Current Practices/Opinions

Here you build on what you have presented in the background section. You have already defined the issues or the problems, you have put them in historical contexts, and explained existing perspectives and approaches. You have also discussed how similar companies, schools, or districts have been dealing with the same kinds of issues or problems. In this section you go into further detail about the current status of the issue or problem in your company, school, or district. You also provide an overview of current practices by institutions facing the same or similar problems or issues. In your formal paper or white paper you will review optional approaches, perspectives, ideas, and opinions. This is a key element for this section of your formal report or white paper. You need to present these optional approaches, perspectives, and opinions logically and, if possible, in hierarchical order. You need to explain them thoroughly and very specifically so that your audience will clearly understand each of them, be able to react to them, to think about them, and to ponder them. Intrinsically in this section you are also presenting evidence for your conclusions and recommendations.

You should also comment on the viability of each of the optional approaches, perspectives, ideas, and opinions in terms of their strengths and their limitations. Through your commentary on these approaches, perspectives, and opinions you are building a case for your conclusions and recommendations. You do this as objectively as possible, but as you do so evidence for your own choices could become apparent. You are building an evidentiary base for your conclusions and recommendations.

Use formal language in discussing these approaches and opinions, citing, from your sources, the pros and cons of each one. Be sure that each approach or opinion is discussed thoroughly. Use citations from literature reviewed, personal communications, and interviews as you build evidentiary bases for your commentary. You need to remember that you are providing, in this section, a strong evidentiary base for your conclusions and recommendations. When this section of your white paper or formal report, you are ready for the final section which consists of conclusions and recommendations.

Conclusions and Recommendations

This is the last section of your formal paper or white paper. This is the part of the paper where you bring together everything you have presented about current practices, perspectives, and opinions to develop and present your conclusions and recommendations.

Your purpose was to inform a specific audience about a defined issue or problem You know your audience and you need to consider the needs of your audience as you develop your conclusions and recommendations. Your conclusions are based on the evidence you have built in the previous sections of your formal paper or white paper. If the evidence is strong and specific and illuminates the issue or problem, your conclusions and recommendations will be sound and functional. Your readers, by the time they come to this section of your report or white paper, should have a clear understanding of your conclusions and your recommendations. The audience knows you have defined the problem, discussed the background and current issues, understand the evidentiary bases, and be comfortable with the conclusions and recommendations.

This section is brief. You simply state what your conclusions and your recommendation in language similar to this: "Based on the review of current practices and opinions, I have concluded that. . . ." You use the same language for recommendations: "Based on the review of current practices and opinions and on my conclusions, I recommend that. . . ." You may come to more than one conclusion and more than one recommendation. List them sequentially. Do not comment on nor embellish either the conclusions or the recommendations. If you have written the background and current practices, perspectives, and opinions sections soundly and clearly with evidence and specificity, you will only need to list your conclusions and your recommendations. When this section is completed you have finished your formal paper or white paper. Congratulations.

Writing Tips

Remember that you must follow the APA format and style. You are writing a formal report/white paper and you write it within the parameters of formal writing conventions. Use only the past and present perfect tenses in all sections of your paper. You may write the conclusions in present tense, though present perfect tense is acceptable. Follow all the grammatical expectations of formal writing. Use an economy of expression. Say only what needs to be said. Write predominantly in direct declarative simple sentences. Check the sections in this *Handbook* which deal with with these issues. Make sure the paper reads well. One way to ensure this is to read it aloud. You will hear, as you read, any writing problems in the paper.

The length of a formal report or white paper depends on the nature of the problem or issue, the audience for which it is written, and the purpose of the paper. You may divide the paper into the sections noted earlier. Instead of introduction, the full title of the report or paper is provided. The next sections are titled background, current practices and conclusions and recommendations. In most instances you will not need to include a table of contents. For longer reports and white papers you may want to include a table of contents as well as a review of literature as major sections of the paper. If you need a review of literature, you must have at least two categories. If subcategories are needed, you must have at least two. Be sure to refer to those sections in this *Handbook* if they are required or expected for your report or white paper. For a quick review of the expectations for writing formal reports or white papers, refer to the checklist on page 123.

14 Preparing a Guidebook or Handbook

You may, in your professional career, be assigned to write a guidebook or a handbook. The purpose of a guidebook is to provide for the reader a step by step process for putting together a product, delineating a process, or developing a set of directions for how to do a task or series of tasks. A guidebook or handbook consists of a sequential series of steps developed to instruct readers on how to complete a task, learn a process, or achieve the objectives described sequentially in the purpose of the handbook. A guidebook or handbook is generally written in narrative form with each step in the sequence explained thoroughly, clearly, and as succinctly as possible. A guidebook or handbook should serve an identified audience and should include clear, sequential, and specific directions for the process of developing a product, learning a process, or completing a task.

Organization

You should provide for the readers an introduction in which you explain the purpose of the handbook and introduce the materials needed and why they are important. Back up information and references could also be included in your guidebook. References are placed in a reference section immediately following the narrative. Back up information should be included in appendixes so they will not impede the process, but would be available

> *A guidebook or handbook is generally written in narrative form with each step in the sequence explained thoroughly, clearly, and as succinctly as possible.*

to the reader for more detailed information. Appendixes are placed at the end of the handbook following the references.

You must write your guidebook or handbook clearly and concisely with each step clearly explained. This economy of expression and clarity of language are essential in preparing a guidebook or a handbook. Many guidebooks or handbooks fail because the language is too technical or too obtuse. In these instances readers do not easily follow the guidebook and can become confused about the process. Readers should not have to struggle to interpret your directions and the sequential steps. A guidebook or handbook is not designed to illustrate your technical knowledge nor your sophisticated and esoteric language. It must be clear and concise. Your guidebook or handbook will usually contain a table of contents which follows the guidelines in this *Handbook* (pages 5 and 6). The table of contents includes a listing of all categories or steps and, if needed, subcategories or sub steps.

Additional support information and directions are placed in appendixes. Appendixes contain information and specifics too detailed to be included in the guidebook or handbook. Your appendix will include supplementary material related to the process outlined in the guidebook. All materials in the appendix are keyed to specific steps in the guidebook or handbook and provide necessary backup material for the users. Information in the appendixes, like narrative materials in the handbook itself, follow APA guidelines and are written, for the most part, in the past or present perfect tense. Conventions of formal grammar and formal writing conventions are followed in preparing your guidebook or handbook. If needed, you will include a reference section following the narrative in the guidebook. References are those resources cited in the guidebook and in the appendix. In the appendix additional information and evidence will be provided for the readers so they can gain a more complete understanding of the product or the process.

Writing Tips

Your handbook follows the conventions of formal writing. The APA format is used in preparing your guidebook. It is important that you write clearly and concisely in providing directions and steps in the process. Use short declarative simple sentences in your narrative. Follow the conventions of formal grammar. Make sure that, in the appendix, you provide a clear explanation of backup materials necessary for interpreting sequential steps and for a better understanding of each of the steps. Sometimes in writing guidebooks or handbooks there is a tendency to assume a certain level of understanding in your audience. Make no such assumptions. The language must be clear, be concise, and easily understood. The steps must be sequential with logical transitions from step to step. To ensure that you have completed all components expected within the handbook, refer to the checklist on page 124.

Preparing a Staff Development Program

15

Preparing a staff development program is a professional responsibility. It begins with a needs assessment and includes identifying outcomes, determining personnel needed and their roles, gathering resources, developing a specific plan for the program, sequencing activities, involving participants the activities, and evaluating the outcomes. These are the essential components of preparing a staff development program and must be thoughtfully considered and carefully planned to ensure the success of the program.

Needs Assessment

Before you actually begin specific planning of your staff development program it is wise and usually necessary to do a needs assessment to determine the interest and skill level of the participants in terms of the content of the staff development program. A needs assessment can help you learn what the participants feel they need, and the kind of outcomes they expect from the staff development program. A needs assessment should be a straightforward questionnaire or survey designed to determine level of knowledge and skills in the area of the proposed program. A five or six point semantic differential scale could also be used as part of the survey to determine knowledge and levels of achievement. Skills to be included in the program could be listed along with participant's level of knowledge and

A needs assessment should be a straightforward questionnaire or survey designed to determine level of knowledge and skills in the area of the proposed program.

understanding included in the semantic differential. Outcomes about what the attendee would expect to learn in terms of the objectives should be included in the survey. It is wise to put a copy of the needs assessment in an appendix.

It is important to keep the survey relatively brief. The survey should, if possible, be no more than one page in length and should be easy to complete. The format should be inviting and attractive. It needs to be distributed at least several days before the staff developed program is scheduled. In this way you will have time to very specifically plan the staff development based, for the most part, on the needs assessment. The analysis of the survey results is integral to the planning of the staff development program. In the final evaluation of the staff development the survey and the analysis of the results should be included in an appendix following the evaluation report.

Identifying Outcomes

Analysis of the survey or questionnaire needs to be thoughtfully and carefully done. This analysis is vital to planning for the success of the staff development program. You cannot really plan goals, expected outcomes and the skills developed during the program without careful analysis of the needs assessment survey or questionnaire. After the analysis of the needs assessment the planning process begins with identifying the expected outcomes of the program. Differentiated outcomes need to be considered based on the responses to the needs assessment. Differentiated outcomes need to be listed along with processes for their achievement. The planner first needs to consider the needs of the participant and their perceived outcomes of the staff development. Once this has been done you should relate those stated needs and those expected outcomes to your planning of the outcomes of the staff development program. Based on perceived needs and expected outcomes, those participating in the staff development activities may need to have differentiated instruction and participative interaction. Planning should incorporate the need for differentiated areas of focus and differentiated outcomes where necessary. Identifying outcomes requires thoughtful and careful consideration of the information gained from the needs assessment.

Personnel

The question of selecting personnel for the staff development program is an important component of the overall planning process. You need to develop a list of people who will organize the program, present the program, fill support roles, develop sequence of activities, be responsible for involving participants, do the evaluation, and those who will fill ancillary service roles. Include job descriptions where necessary. All of these roles must be considered. Depending however, on the number of participants and the kind of activities included, these roles could all be filled by a few individuals. For larger numbers of participants and a large number of activities, you may need multiple personnel for some or many of these roles. Your identification and placement of participating personnel should be based on the needs assessment and on your definition of the expected outcomes of the staff development program.

Organizing the Program

This is primarily your responsibility. You may, however, wish to delegate this responsibility to another person. Within this organizational process you need to outline the components of the program and put into them as much detail as needed. Design any workshops within the program as well as any specialized differentiated activities to meet the needs of the participants. Develop time frames for each activity and the content of each component. Make sure you plan for transitions, breaks, as well as snacks, lunch, or dinner You need to carefully build a sequence of activities that will build toward an effective conclusion and a strong evaluation. All of this information should be written into your planning narrative for the program.

Presenters

Presenting personnel are very important to the success of the program. It is essential that strong presenters be selected to lead all workshops in the program. You should review the qualifications of possible presenters and check on how they have done in previous presentations on the subject. If possible, it is wise to choose respected members of the company or school district to which participants are assigned. These presenters are often known to the participants and have either the authority of leadership or the professional respect of the participants. If they possess both, so much the better. If you have workshops or hands on activities built into the presentation you need to get the best people possible to lead those interactive groups or workshops. Selecting peers, if possible, is a good way of providing such leadership.

Plan for an evaluator or an identified person to be responsible for evaluation. Evaluation consists of a summary or review of the program which could be done interactively with participants. Then the participants complete an evaluation form. The evaluator should attend the large group formal presentation, walk through and observe small group activities and workshops, and interact with participants wherever possible. The evaluator summarizes the program, which can be presented or discussed interactively with the participants. The evaluator distributes and collects the evaluation form. You and the evaluator are then responsible for the analysis of the evaluation form and the preparation of a final report. You may also want to include the presenters, the activity/workshop leaders, and other personnel in the preparation of the final report. All personnel involved in the program need to provide an assessment of the quality of their participation and the completion of their roles.

In addition to the professional presenters, workshop/activity leaders, and evaluator, there are other personnel roles to consider. You need to determine who will register the participants, who will set up the area for all activities, who will decorate the activity areas if needed, who will ensure that snacks, lunch, or dinner are prepared and served. You will need to identify those who are responsible for any technology and other materials needed for the program and who is responsible for set up and removal of materials. You will also need to identify human resources for equipment breakdowns, spills, health issues, and emergency procedures. Including all of these personnel issues is essential to the success of the program.

Resources

You should make a list of necessary resources needed for the program. This will include technology resources, print resources including handbooks and support materials, supplies and equipment for workshops or activities, writing pads and pens/pencils for taking notes, and other resources that may be needed for ensuring the success of the program. Be sure these are all in place by the beginning of the workshop. Seating arrangements and areas for small group activities need to be determined.

Planning for Differentiated Needs

From the needs assessment you have found that there are a number of needs expressed by participants. These may require differentiated needs. You should prepare for those needs by designing activities and workshops in small group settings to meet those needs. This is very important if you wish to have participants have an optimum learning experience. There could be a series of activities or workshops through which participants could be involved. If, for example, you plan three activities for each participant these could be arranged in an hierarchical progression designed to meet the needs of identified participants.

Involving Participants

For most staff development programs it is important to involve participants in a variety of differentiated activities and/or workshops. You need to plan for small group focused activities or workshops. You need to make them, in many instances hands on group activities. They could also be discussion groups. You could even have the activities involve both discussion and hands on. Participants need to have an interactive context in most staff development programs. If participants can leave the program with some kind of product, it can be a real plus for the participants. Interactive involvement with defined outcomes leads toward a more positive evaluation.

Evaluation

Evaluation, as already noted, should be a defined personnel position. You may fill that role as the coordinator and developer or you may select another person to fill this role. The evaluator should attend all large group sessions, visit each workshop or activity, interact with as many participants as possible, ask questions, and take notes. The evaluator should be on the program as the last presenter. The evaluator should review the presentations, the workshops/activities, and provide some of the comments obtained earlier by interaction with the participants. These comments should, for the most part, be positive. In some instances the comments from participants could touch on ideas for followup programs, how to use the material learned, and what were the most valuable parts of the program. After the summary presentation which could also be done interactively, the evaluator then introduces the evaluation form. The evaluation form could include an overall evaluation of the program using a semantic differential. It could also include checklists on what elements of the program could be implemented or used by the participants. The most valuable components of the program and what might be changed if the program were used again could be included. Each workshop or activity in which the participant was part of the group should be evaluated. This could be done either at the end of the program or at the close of each of the activities. The evaluation form should be kept as simple as possible. Keep it to one page if you can. Be sure it is anonymous, although some demographic data such as department, school, or assignment could be incorporated at the beginning of the evaluation form. You, the evaluator, and other identified personnel are responsible for writing the final report of the program.

Writing Tips

When writing your staff development program you need to include information about all of the components listed above. You are writing this staff development program in narrative form. In writing your report on the program you follow the conventions of formal writing. You use the past or present perfect tense. You follow the APA guidelines for formal writing as well as using this *Handbook*. Your report should be clearly and concisely written. In your report you will address each of the components of the program and discuss each. You will include results of the evaluation form for each component of the program. Each of the components could be a category for your report. Remember to use an economy of expression. If the report is lengthy, prepare a table of contents. Be aware of the audience for the program. It could go only to supervisors, to executives of the company or school district, to the participants, or to all of the above. All or part of the evaluation report could go to participants. You, as developer and coordinator of the program, can make that choice. It is good to inform participants, in some way, the results of the evaluation. Strongly consider this as a part of your evaluation report. You can choose to share the whole report or parts of the report. For a quick review of the components of staff development programs see the checklist on page 125.

16 Preparing Program Evaluations

Every program, project, theme or unit, and intervention needs to be evaluated. You can do an evaluation through qualitative or quantitative research or you can evaluate programs, projects, units, and other interventions through an identified process. The focus in this section of the *Handbook* is on evaluation through an identified process, although there is a category in this section on research.

Overview

Evaluation is the process of reviewing a program to determine its effectiveness and to determine whether it should be continued or terminated. This is a necessary process and one which is sensitive because it involves personnel, stakeholders, and the company, school, or school district in which the program is functioning. There are two kinds of program reviews. One is done by personnel within the company, the school, or the school district and the second is an outside evaluation done by evaluators not associated with the company, the school, or the school district.

There are two major kinds of program reviews. There is the program quality review designed to determine the quality and value of the program. In addition, there are compliance reviews which could also be done from within the company, the school, or the school district or they could be done

> *Evaluation is the process of reviewing a program to determine its effectiveness and to determine whether it should be continued or terminated.*

by outside evaluators. Compliance reviews are designed to determine whether the program is following the state and federal guidelines required by the funding source. Compliance reviews are required by most funding sources. Private funding sources can also require compliance reviews. Because compliance reviews are specific to the funding source, they are not central to this work. The focus here is on program quality review. Funded programs programs usually have a designated time frame ranging from one year to up to five years. These kinds of program reviews are done annually beginning with the first year. Programs which are funded by the companies or by school districts generally follow the same or similar evaluation processes.

In many instances evaluations of programs are done by a team of evaluators. There is usually a lead evaluator and along with other members of the team who may specialize in particular aspects of the program being evaluated. The evaluators work as a team and develop strategies, sequences, and activities for the evaluators. They study the program, identify the expected outcomes, review the processes involved, and review the written program evaluation. They interview participants, observe the program in action, review written materials from the project. In some instances in funded programs with limited budgets the evaluation is done by a single evaluator, often from the project itself. In those instances, the evaluation form and process is defined by the funding source. For our purposes we are considering only those evaluations involving a team.

Background Information

Before the program evaluation actually begins you and your team, as evaluators, should receive the annual reports about the function and results of the program. Be sure to require all annual reports from the inception of the program. These reports should include program benchmarks and objectives, a detailed budget, program timelines and activities, personnel, tests and evaluation measures, and results of those tests and evaluations. Evaluations and program outcomes are particularly important. The most recent program evaluation is essential to the evaluation process. Also needed are program goals and objectives for the next year along with a projected budget. Program managers should, in addition, provide you with a list of stakeholders including employees, consultants, parents, students, members of boards or advisory councils, and any others that may be pertinent to the operation of the program. Be sure to contact the program managers and identify the information you and your team will need. Discuss the time frame for the evaluating the program and the components of the program. The program evaluation, particularly from the most recent year, is essential for conducting the evaluation.

The timeline for the evaluation needs to be developed before the evaluation begins. Identify the components and plan for time frames for each. Time should be allocated for an open meeting with program managers and personnel, observations of operations or classroom observations, and interviews with program managers, program personnel, participants, and stakeholders. Questions should be prepared for interviews. Identify what needs to be seen in the observations. Time for writing and preparing the final report also needs to be included in the timeline. As noted, be sure to discuss the timeline with program managers and make any adjustments related to schedules that may be needed. Do not leave out any of the components noted because of scheduling problems. Remember that most program evaluations generally take more than one day. Plan schedules for the time needed. Generally major program reviews take about three to four days.

Steps in the Evaluation Process

After you have completed your timeline, contacted the program managers, and made any adjustments necessary, the evaluation process can begin. When you and your team arrive, you first meet with the program managers and finalize the schedule for the program review. Hold an open meeting to share this information, discuss the process, and indicate the time for the final meeting. After the open meeting observations take place. This is followed by interviews with program managers, personnel, and stakeholders. At the close of each day the team should meet to share notes, discuss issues, and work on the preparation of the final report. Discussion should focus on the strengths of the program, identified limitations, and the relationship of what is observed and interview results in the context of program objectives. In the second and third day this process continues with the progressive writing of the final report. On the final day of the evaluation the final report is completed and presented in an open meeting including program personnel, participants, and stakeholders.

Writing the Final Report

Because you are writing a report that will be publicly heard and usually read verbatim, you need to consider the writing process carefully. Your report should include a brief statement about the nature of the program and how it has developed and changed from its inception, the objectives of the program, and progress toward the achievement of the objectives. Generally you are evaluating during the actual implementation of the program and where it is. Yours is not an end of year report. That is done by the program managers and is reported to the funding source. Your report should reflect the actuality of what was observed, the feelings and attitudes of the managers, personnel, participants, and stakeholders. You will report the strengths of the program and the positive elements within it. You will also define limitations and areas that need to be changed or improved. Your evaluation report is a critique of the program from the perspectives of your team. Much of it will be positive, yet the report needs to include recommendations for change and improvement. You will develop a rich, thick narrative of what you observed, your interviews with managers, personnel, and stakeholders. You can include pertinent comments from your interviews as appropriate.

You then, from the evidence provided, develop conclusions and make recommendations. Generally these will be positive, but within them you can conclude that certain things need to be adjusted or changed and recommend a process for making those changes. These conclusions are what the program managers, personnel, and stakeholders have been waiting for. When you write these, they should be carefully wrought, but straightforward and to the point. It is your task as evaluators to give a sound professional judgment as to the quality of the program and make suggestions for changes and adjustments to improve the program. It should be noted that you may cite sources to provide additional evidence for your conclusions and recommendations. These citations can be placed in any section of the report as long as they are pertinent and do not impede the clarity of the report.

You should also meet with program managers daily to ensure that you are gathering all the necessary information, seeing all the important activities, and interviewing stakeholders pertinent to the program. The program managers need to be informed. They need to keep you and your team informed and provide any information the team may need. Always plan to review the final report with the program managers before it is read publicly. This is important because the managers need to know what is being presented. They may even suggest editorial changes if time permits. They may also provide responses to the recommendations which can informally be presented at the open meeting if appropriate.

In the open meeting the report is usually read verbatim by the reviewers to ensure that there is no mistake or misunderstanding by the audience. Copies of the report may be made for the program personnel or stakeholders. After the report has been presented, the program managers may want to make a brief statement. Allow for this. Thank the managers, the personnel, and the stakeholders for their participation in the evaluation and then allow for questions. The time for questions should be relatively brief. Additional questions can be referred to the managers and personnel who can, at a later time, receive your responses to the questions.

Writing Tips

We have briefly reviewed the process and have discussed the writing of the report. It should be remembered that the APA format and style should be followed. Your report should have these sections: Program summary, program objectives, program operations and personnel, and conclusions and recommendations. These are the categories you will consider.

You may title them differently depending on the program. You may write your formal paper or white paper as a narrative without the use of formal categories. In doing so, however, you need to include the sections noted above. Be sensitive to the needs of your audience and utilize the most effective organization you can to meet those needs. You will also want to include in the program summary a brief history of the program. You will include pertinent citations and follow the narrative with the reference section. Write clearly and concisely and use an economy of expression. Use, for the most part, simple declarative sentences. For a quick review of the components of program evaluation see checklist on page 126.

17 Preparing a Grant Proposal

Grant proposals must be developed according to the guidelines and format of the request for proposals (RFP). These are provided by the funding source. In the RFP there is an expectation for a statement of need, the goals and objectives of the proposed program, a time line for the implementation and achievement of those goals and objectives, a budget for funding the proposed program, and personnel necessary for program operation. Each RFP will have these basic components. Additional components, information and legal requirements would be specified in the RFP.

In preparing your grant proposal you would first specifically describe the problem or issue being addressed and the interventions you are proposing. You will need to define the problems, the need for change, and the importance of the interventions. You will specifically note the needs addressed and how the interventions relate to the identified needs. To do this you may need, if space permits, to cite sources that both substantiate the need and identify the importance of the interventions. This must be done specifically and in some detail so that the readers of the proposal can clearly understand what your problems are and how you are going to intervene to address and resolve the problem. You must use an economy of expression and say only what needs to be said.

You will also need to prepare broad program goals which clarify program purpose and support the interventions planned. Goals are broad general statements of outcomes. Goals are your generic expectations. They should be supported by

> Grant proposals must be developed according to the guidelines and format of the request for proposals (RFP).

specific measurable objective that are keyed to each of the needs you have already stated. The measurable objectives should be directly related to a timeline during a designated time of program operation. Benchmarks and identified products and outcomes should be fitted into the timeline so that readers can clearly note the sequence and process involved in the program. This is important because readers need to be able to easily identify the objectives and the timeline and be able to understand the process involved in the program interventions.

It is important to identify personnel needed to operate the program. Personnel could include managers, support personnel, certificated personnel, and classified personnel. Where necessary job descriptions or personnel roles could be provided. Personnel information should be included in the appropriate section of the narrative expectations within the RFP. You should note the stakeholders in appropriate categories of the RFP. Stakeholders could include those served, parents, and the community.

You will need also to prepare a budget for your grant proposal. Budgets should include seven categories: First (1000), a category for certificated personnel. Second (2000), a category for classified personnel. Third (3000), a category for benefits such as social security and workmen's compensation. Fourth (4000), a category for supplies and equipment. Fifth (5000), a category for operations. Sixth (6000) a category for capital outlay such as computers and technology. Seventh (7000), a category for indirect costs such as electricity, rent, and custodial services. Your company or school district usually charges a fixed percent for indirect costs These are most of the components of a budget. Budgets not specific to education may have a slightly different set of budget categories. Your RFP will provide specific guidelines for budget preparation.

Be sure to carefully review the RFP for compliance issues which you will need to address. Include any other requests for information such as demographic data and inclusive dates of the program if designed for multi year operation. Include any additional information that may be needed by the funding source. Among this information should be demographic data relating both to program personnel and program participants. These are the basic components that need to be addressed when writing a grant proposal. It is wise to have others review your proposal to ensure clarity and logical development.

Writing Tips

Your first obligation is to follow the requirements and categories of the RFP as they are identified and defined in the document. You need to follow the directions within each category very specifically. For narrative portions of the grant proposal follow the format and guidelines of the APA. Syntax is very important in grant proposals. You must use, for the most part, short declarative sentences in the active voice. Be straightforward and honest in what you say. Make sure that the language is clear and that the elements and narratives in the grant proposal are logical in their progression and follow each other sequentially both in terms of narrative and the completion of the material required by the funding source. Remember that you will have other professionals competing for funding. Your proposal must follow the conventions of formal writing and the expectations of the funding source. Best wishes. For a quick review of the expectations for grant writing see the checklist on page 127.

18

Preparing an Action Research Study

Chapter

Action research refers to an individual doing research with a small population. The population could be one person or it could be up to thirty or more. Action research is generally qualitative research, though it could be quantitative or a combination of both research paradigms. Essentially action research involves a manager or a teacher who develops and implements an intervention with people in a defined group. Action research can be done with one person or one student. When this happens, action research can also be termed single case research.

The general purpose of action research is to find out how an intervention works with a relatively small group of people or students. Preparing an action research project is somewhat less structured than a formal qualitative or quantitative study. There are, however, some parameters within which the researcher must work. In writing an action research project you must first clearly enunciate the purpose of the study including objectives and expected outcomes. Second, you need to identify the need for and the rationale for the action research. Third, you need to identify the intervention clearly and succinctly. Fourth, you need to specify how you plan to implement the research and prepare an activity timeline for the study. Fifth, you need to provide an evaluation design to show how you are going to determine the outcomes or results of the intervention.

> *The general purpose of action research is to find out how an intervention works with a relatively small group of people or students.*

Purpose

You need to clearly state the purpose of your action research. The reader needs to know this at the beginning of your action research study. You, as the researcher, must be very clear about this and specifically state it. An opening statement such as: "The purpose of this action research was to. . . ." Then specify your purpose and add the objectives of the action research. Objectives need to be measurable and either behaviorally oriented or involve changing a process, changing attitudes, or utilizing the learnings from the planned intervention. The objectives will vary somewhat depending on whether this is a single case research study or involves a somewhat larger group. The purpose and the objectives are important components of your action research. State them clearly and succinctly.

Rationale

Early in your document you need to identify the rationale for research. You need to tell the reader why you are doing the research. The question of why the research is needed is one you should answer early in your action research proposal. The need for the research must be apparent and substantive. The rationale could have two dimensions. First, the importance of the topic in the field needs to be stated. Second, the importance of the topic to the population involved. The perspectives on rationale need to be explained and at least one needs to be included in your document. You may focus on the more localized of the rationales, or on the wider importance of the topic to the field. You may even include both of them in your document. You need to cite some sources for your rationale and for your intervention. Include a reference page for resources you have cited. For action research you do not necessarily need a review of literature. You do, however need to cite pertinent resources in the field that relate directly to the question addressed in the study.

Intervention

Your intervention needs to be clearly and succinctly stated. The intervention needs to be defined and linked to the purpose of the research, to the rationale, and to the stated objectives of the study. You need to be clear and concise in your definition of the problem and provide information about how the intervention will be implemented, monitored, and administered. Here again you also need to cite resources in order to support the professionalism of the intervention. Your intervention needs to be sound, as simple as possible, and be designed to meet the objectives and the identified needs.

Implementation

It is important to define implementation in terms of process and activities. You will need to provide an expected timeline for each activity. You will need to address the process of implementation and any differentiation in the intervention as the research progresses. A timeline of the components of the intervention activities needs to be developed and followed. Adjustments could be made as necessary based on participant responses to the interventions. It is important to identify benchmarks and link evaluation strategies to the the implementation and associated timeline. In many instances, particularly in single case action research, you need to keep an anecdotal record of what happened during the implementation. In larger studies you need to observe events, define and discuss changes in the participants, and keep accurate and objective records about the process of implementation and change. Implementation is the centerpiece of your action research and you must keep accurate records about how the process was implemented, noting the activities and benchmarks, and recording the results of the activities resulting in benchmarks.

Evaluation

Your should, in your action research, have a well defined evaluation design. You may use observation and anecdotal records. You may also use pre and posttests. You could interview participants and you could use a survey or questionnaire. You could use performance based tasks or creation of defined products There are, of course, other evaluation strategies that could be used. You need to select those most pertinent to your research. Regardless of the evaluation design, you should use it in a way that will demonstrate to the reader what changes occurred through the intervention. If you used tests, surveys, or interviews the results will give you and the reader a perspective on the effect of the intervention. If you are using a survey, you can use descriptive statistical measures to determine outcomes. Descriptive statistical measures most generally used are mean, median, mode, range, and standard deviation. If you use anecdotal records, they must be complete and provide the necessary detail to indicate the impact of the intervention on the participant(s). Evaluation is very important and the results need to be shared and publicized. This is especially true if you want to have the intervention replicated by others. Do not neglect to write conclusions and recommendations for your action research study.

Once these five steps have been accomplished, you have completed your action research study. Action research is something a professional can do. You can do it in your department or in your classroom You can use it with one person or with a group of people. Action research is something you can do without depending on consultants of any kind. Inform your supervisor, obtain permission to do the study, identify what you want to do, plan specifically and sequentially, and follow the steps described above. Implement confidently, keep track of what you do, have a strong evaluation plan, and determine the results of the intervention carefully. Consider whether your action research could be replicated. If so, write a thorough report and share it with company or school district personnel.

Writing Tips

Action research is less formal that qualitative or quantitative research. It is done on a small scale and with limited personnel. When writing your action research proposal, you need to follow APA guidelines. Write crisply and cogently. Use short declarative simple sentences for the most part. The past tense and present perfect tense should be used most of the time because when you write the report the research has been completed. You will be citing some sources, even though you do not have a review of literature. Be sure to follow APA guidelines for these. Include a reference page. It is important to use an economy of expression. Make every word count and choose the right word to illuminate meaning. Your purpose is to tell the story of your research clearly and concisely, but with enough detail to make it a professional representation of what you planned, what you did, how you did it, and the results achieved in your study. For a quick review of the expectations for preparing an action research study see the checklist on page 128.

19 Preparing Curriculum

Creating or developing a curriculum, while focused on education, can be applied to any instructional sequence required for new employees, for retraining, or for developing new skills for groups of people. There are a number of steps involved in preparing curriculum. Among these are selecting standards, identifying objectives, creating a time frame, deciding what classroom structure to use, determining primary materials for the curriculum, choosing technology if needed, determining the level of cognition to be achieved, identifying teaching strategies, deciding on assessment practices, and developing an instructional sequence. If you have members in your class who have a home language other than English, you will also select identified specially designed activities in English (SDAIE) as well as providing for a reflection or review of how the lessons worked with the students. Each of these categories is defined and explained in this narrative.

First, however, you will need to prepare an introduction to the curriculum in which you note the purpose of the curriculum unit, theme, or area of focus. In the introduction you will also need to identify the importance of the curriculum. Here you may cite some sources and follow the style and format of the APA for those citations and for the narrative. The final component of the introduction is the rationale for preparing the curriculum. Why you chose it and why you detailed the specific area of focus or content. These three items complete the introduction. You will also need to have a title page for the curriculum. For the

You should be familiar with the standards in your own state and use them for planning your own curriculum.

introduction and the title page follow the instructions in the *Handbook*. You may need to include a table of contents in the curriculum package. Again, follow the instructions in the *Handbook*.

Selecting Standards

Standards are provided for schools in every state. One state calls them learning expectations. In a more generic sense, standards provide the expectations for students to be able to demonstrate when the curriculum is completed. If you are teaching in a school you need to be aware of the standards provided by your state department of education. Standards or expectations are also used by companies or other institutions to reflect minimum skills needed for certain jobs or activities. You will need to select a standard for each instructional lesson. Sometimes more than one standard can be selected. However, usually one standard can be used for each lesson. In a longer sequence of lessons, several standards could be used. Remember that standards are constant. They are the expectations toward which you are working in terms of your instruction. In education there are standards for every grade level and for every content area. There are slightly different formats, names of content areas, and structures in each state. You should be familiar with the standards in your own state and use them for planning your own curriculum.

Identifying Objectives

After you have selected the standard or standards you are working toward, you need to identify the specific objectives for the lesson or lessons you are teaching. Your objectives should be behavioral. This means that within the objectives behavior outcomes are noted. Behaviors, skills or processes should be noted in the objectives. Objectives should be brief and to the point. They should reflect what you feel the outcomes of the lesson should be. You may use only one objective or you may include more than one objective for a specific lesson. In writing your objective, conceptualize what you want the students to learn, to be able to do or demonstrate, or what they will be able to build or create. Take real care in preparing your objectives. They are essential to the success of your lesson. It is always important for students to be aware of both the standard toward which they are working and of the objectives they are expected to achieve by the end of the lesson or lessons. If you have a series of lessons on a particular topic, plan objectives for each lesson. They should be linked together and built on each other. In cases where there are a series of lessons, objectives can change based on the results of each lesson. Objectives change depending on how students have reacted to individual lessons. Lessons later in a sequence of lessons may need to be changed as students learning is demonstrated. Be prepared to make any necessary changes in objectives.

Time Frame

In your planning consider the time it will take to achieve the objectives you have planned. Each individual lesson should have a time frame ranging from a few minutes to a period or even to a workshop of one or two days. You need to gauge the amount of time needed for the students to demonstrate that they have achieved the objective or the measures implied in the standard. Approach the time frame thoughtfully. If there are a series of lessons related to specific objectives, note how much time is needed and for how many periods or days are needed in the sequence of lessons. Sometimes the time frame is dictated by the schedule of allocated time in terms of periods or a specific beginning and ending time. You need to develop the time frame keeping within any parameters and ensuring that you will have enough time to achieve the objectives in your lesson or lessons.

Classroom Structures

Classroom structures indicate how you are going to organize for teaching. There are many ways to structure your classroom. You can use whole group instruction through direct instruction or you may use a wide variety of group structures. Some group structures that could be used include pairs, triads, cooperative groups, dialectic groups, jigsaws, and many others. Steinaker and Leavitt (2008) identify many group structures, define them, and show how they can be used in the classroom. You can also use a combination of structures. For example you may wish to start with whole group instruction so that students will gain some basic knowledge of the subject and be introduced to the standards, the objectives of the lesson, study, or workshop. You can also provide any basic information the students need including a time frame and schedule. Following whole group instruction, you may wish to break the class into cooperative groups or other kinds of groups. Groups can be assigned the same task or each group can have a different assignment. You make the choice. Groups should be carefully planned, have defined tasks, and be monitored by the teacher or by assigned assistant teachers. When group work has been completed or when the time frame for group work is completed, the class can be called together for sharing and evaluation. You have real flexibility in planning your classroom structures. Choose those you feel will work best for the participants.

Primary Program Materials

You will be using specific materials for your lesson or lessons. You need to note the materials you will be using with your students. Among the materials you could use with your students are district adopted basal materials or textbooks. You may also use trade books or supplemental texts. You may use newspapers, journals, or magazine. Realia or hands-on materials can be used. Handbooks or guidebooks can also be used. In many instances you could use audiovisual materials or computer programs. You need to select those materials that would be most helpful to you and your students in achieving the stated objectives of the lesson or lessons. Select the materials carefully and be sure that you can access the materials and that there are enough to serve all your students. You need to make sure that the materials can be read and understood by the students or participants. Wherever possible you should review the materials and become familiar with them before you use them with students or participants. Understand when they will be used in the lessons, why they were chosen, how they relate to the lessons, and how they will be used.

Group Structures

You need to consider how you will group your students during the course of the lesson. There are many group structures you can use. You may even use more than one group structure depending on the nature of the lesson. Group structures can be whole group instruction, cooperative learning groups or a number of other group structures. Among the other group structures are pairs, triads, numbered groups, single focus groups, planning groups, jigsaw groups, and dialectic groups where two or more ideas or points of view are given and the group comes to a consensus about the perspective they feel is most appropriate. There are other group structures that you can use (Steinaker & Leavitt, 2008). We want to emphasize the value and importance of interactive learning through group structures. It is through interactive learning that students become engaged and where learning is augmented.

Technology

Technology is a tool for learning, but in the context of many schools, districts, and business organizations it is a vitally important tool. You are to select the primary technology you will be using along with other support technologies. Among the technologies you could use are computers, keyboards, overheads, slide projectors, film projectors, compact disks, video disks, calculators, television, radio, and podcasts. There are other technologies that you could also use. Students can create films, develop power point presentations. You may use more than one technology in your program or lessons. When using technology, you should explain how it is used and how it relates to the objectives of the lesson or lessons. If participants are to use the technology, be sure they know how to use it and can function well with it. Provide any assistance or support that may be needed.

Cognitive Levels

In any lesson you need to be aware of the levels of cognition and your expectations for students to achieve as high a level of cognition you have planned for the lesson or lessons. There are seven levels of cognition. They are memory, translation, interpretation, application, analysis, synthesis, and evaluation. For memory an objective can be written using these terms: Defines, identifies, names, describes, lists, and remembers. For translation the operant words are matches, grasps, tells, understands. Interpretation means explaining or summarizing, interpreting material, predicting outcomes or effects, and estimating future trends. Objectives at interpretation can be written using terms such as convert, defend, distinguish, estimate, explain, generalize, rewrite, give examples. For application students use material in new concrete situations and apply rules, methods, laws, and theories. Words for objectives are changes, computes, uses, demonstrates, solves, shows, operates, applies. Analysis means breaking into parts, organizing materials to establish criteria, clarifying and drawing conclusions. Descriptors for objectives are breaks out, outlines, discriminates, subdivides, compares, organizes, distinguishes, diagrams, relates, and contrasts. Synthesis relates to preparing a unique communication, developing a set of abstract relations, and putting parts together for a new whole. Words used for writing objectives are combines, composes, compiles, creates, designs, rearranges, modifies, develops. The last category of cognition is evaluation. Here students judge value based on established criteria, supports judgment with reason and evidence, and values for specified purpose. Terms used for writing objectives are appraises, critiques, judges, chooses, supports, values, selects, evaluates.

A single lesson should reach the application level of cognition. In a series of lessons you may have lessons in each cognitive level and each lesson should move the students toward the higher levels of cognition.

Teaching Strategies

Teaching strategies are the methodology of instruction. You will need to select teaching strategies that will help ensure student/participant learning. Below we list twenty-five teaching strategies with brief descriptors. For a complete definition of these teaching strategies see Steinaker and Leavitt *Interactive Learning: The Art and Science of Teaching* (2008). Please note the descriptors are not written, in some cases, as complete sentences. The strategies and their descriptors are as follows:

Goal setting: Establishing relationship to previous learning, introducing the lesson. Establishing set and objective.

Data presentation: Providing information, establishing stimuli, identifying resources, using media.

Directed observation: Focusing on particular or selected stimuli, establishing lesson parameters, identifying what to look for.

Data exploration: Student and teacher interacting with the data. Identifying how to find information. Checking for understanding and readiness for next steps in the lesson. Often done interrogatively.

Reflective modeling: Teacher models processes involved in the lesson and interactively with students established clear vision of outcome and how to get there. Students identify relationships to previous learning and respond to known examples.

Generating/using data: Accumulating appropriate resources, generating data, reading, viewing, listening, discussing. Using "why questions, examining additional data.

Unstructured role playing: Providing for role playing and interactive unstructured modeling of student perspectives on the experience. Asking students to show relationships, show a process, or play a role pertinent to the lesson.

Use of manipulatives/realia: Using and exploring realia (hands on artifacts). Involvement in hands-on activities. Learning how to use materials.

Ordering: Sequencing data, arranging data, establishing material hierarchy, defining frames of reference, preparation for guided practice. Also involves checking for understanding.

Selection of data: Selection of needed data and resources for guided practice activities. Focused us of materials. Reading, viewing, working with others.

Using/interpreting data: Using assessing, interpreting data through observing, reading, viewing, and experimenting. Recording data, explaining.

Discussion/interaction: Exchanging information and points of view, questioning, information giving, clarifying. Interaction between teacher/students and students/students. Cooperative groups are appropriate in this strategy.

Hypothesizing: Conceiving and using provisional assumptions as basis for reasoning and action. Conjecturing possible outcomes or possibilities. Developing hypotheses, identifying processes and possible results.

Testing hypotheses: Trying conditional hypotheses in many situations. Applying data, asking questions, confirming or rejective hypotheses, processes, possible outcomes.

Using acquired skills: Use of acquired information and skills. Applying information and skills to problem solving. Demonstrated achievement of lesson objectives.

Observing/sharing: Reviewing processes and sequence of lesson. Sharing, discussing, using and demonstrating learned skills or behaviors. Can also be done in written or multimedia form.

Role playing/simulation: Structures role playing. Overt demonstration of learned skills and roles. Simulation, discussion of outcomes and sharing achievement and success.

Comparing/contrasting: Applying learned skills to new contexts. Analysis of similarities and differences in these new contexts. Can be interrogative and/or interactive.

Summarizing: Reviewing the lesson. Identifying the sequence and process. Developing ideas for reporting and sharing with others.

Reporting: A written, graphic, or multimedia sharing, showing, or explaining the lesson to others.

Presenting: Showing, sharing the experience and its value. Teaching others the processes involved.

Dramatizing: Preparing a skit, play, demonstration. Formalized presentation of the lesson.

Instructing/teaching: Interacting with others about the meaning of the lesson. Can involve peer teaching.

Evaluating: Interactively assessing the meaning of the lesson in terms of developing ideas for new lessons. Looking back on the whole experience, valuing it, and determining new experiences.

These teaching strategies are organized hierarchically. Each five teaching strategies correlate with levels of the interactive taxonomy (Steinaker & Leavitt, 2008). Those levels are information, involvement, investigation, insight, and implementation. You should select several strategies and key them to specific activities in the lesson sequence. Plan them carefully and use them during the delivery of your lesson.

SDAIE Strategies

Specially designed activities in English of SDAIE are strategies and activities you use for students whose home language is other than English and who did not do well on English language development tests They are also good strategies for any learners and can be used with all students. There are many SDAIE strategies. Among them are:

Clustering/semantic mapping: Accessing prior knowledge, reviewing lessons or unit. Using a pre reading activity (clustering). Reviewing a lesson, assessing comprehension (Semantic mapping). A post reading activity.

Cooperative learning: This is also classified as a teaching strategy. A variety of group structures can be used.

Directed reading-thinking activity (DRTA): A pre reading activity involving an interactive dialogue about a story including predicting, reading, discussion, review of predictions, application and analysis.

Found poem: Using a work of literature, document, an original work to help students develop and define personal meaning and interpretation.

Graphic organizers: Organizing information visually. Visually organize and contextualize language. Need to be used in conjunction with direct instruction.

Guided reading: Introduction of reading material including new vocabulary. Discussing story and making predictions.

Interactive writing: Focusing on particular skills in writing, phonics, spelling, grammar, punctuation, editing, revising.

KWL: Focuses students on what they are learning. Students list what they *know*, what they *want* to learn, and on what they have *learned*.

Language experience: A student centered method that uses student language as a basis for reading and writing.

Oral patterned responses: Students respond or generate dialogue using a particular pattern (choral reading, reader's theater).

Print rich environment: Meaningful text posted around the room that students use for information and vocabulary.

Reader's Theater: Teacher or student narrates story as students act it out. Choral reading and student developed skits can be used.

Role playing: Students dramatize situations or stories. This is also classified as a teaching strategy.

Selective listening and "cloze" procedure: Using procedures to check on comprehension and vocabulary. Used to reinforce writing skills. Includes partnering and small group activities. Shared reading: Teacher and students share reading a story, poem, rhyme, and chant.

Shared writing: All students contribute to the writing of a story. Individual students write their own sentences or words.

Think-pair-share: Used in all content areas. Students are to *think* about the question or problem, *pair* up with a partner, and *share* their answers with partner and class.

Writer's workshop: Collaborative approach to the writing process. Students spend time writing and conferencing. Teacher comments on student writing and provides encouragement. Writing is shared and teacher works with students to bring writing to publishing stage.

These are some SDAIE strategies. There are many more. We have provided only brief descriptors of the strategies. We have listed only the most commonly used strategies. When planning a lesson, you need to consider SDAIE strategies and incorporate them in the lesson plan. They are also good strategies that can be used for any students and not just for English learners.

Assessment

Assessment is integral to the success of the lesson. The teacher and the students need to know how well they have learned. Assessment is really the capstone of the lesson plan. Assessments are both short term and long term. Long term assessments are normative tests and criterion referenced tests (CRT). Shorter term assessments are running records (usually for reading and language arts, but could be used in any content area), writing samples, end of chapter or unit tests, demonstrations, use of an oral reading rubric, multimedia reports, teacher made tests, skills tests, and other evaluations. Other evaluations could be observation, interactive discussions, quality of created materials and realia, performance assessments, or group reports. You may use one assessment strategy, but usually you will use more than one strategy. Carefully plan the evaluation measures you will use. Whenever possible have the students demonstrate a learned skill. This can be done in a number of ways including some of the assessment strategies noted above.

Instructional Processes/Outcomes

It is in this category of lesson planning that you prepare a sequence of activities or steps you will follow in the course of the lesson. Each step needs to be delineated and sequenced for clarity of meaning. You may want to share the steps or sequenced with the students so they are aware of the direction of the lesson and your expectations for the achievement of certain benchmarks at specific steps. Be as detailed as is necessary for this sequence of activities. Do not leave out any step or make the steps so broad that they could be interpreted in more than one way. You may want to note how this lesson fits in to a unit of work or an instructional theme. This is the lesson map. Follow the directions you have established in your planning. Share them with the students so they also know expectations and the series of steps you and they will navigate together. This is a vital step and makes the lesson viable for you and the students.

Reflection

In many lessons (hopefully most or all) you will want to reflect on and evaluate what happened in the lesson delivery and what happened in terms of both the process and the achievement of the defined objectives. Did the students achieve the defined objective? Will the skill or process need to be retaught? What parts of the lesson might need reteaching? Were the teaching strategies, SDAIE strategies, and classroom structures appropriate for the lesson? Were the assessments sound? What strategies went right and you will want to use again? These are some of the questions that you may need to consider as you reflect on the results of the lesson. Reflection can also be a basis for next steps and next lessons. It is important that you reflect on your own instruction. This process can be of great use as you seek to become more effective as a teacher.

We have presented a very detailed and specific process for planning, delivering, and evaluating lessons. You need to use something like this for your lesson planning. Two good works that will help provide additional information on lesson planning are Serdyukov and Ryan *A five star approach to lesson planning* (2008) and Steinaker *Heuristic electronic lesson planner* (2007) A third source for lesson planning and analysis can be found in Seinaker and Leavitt (2008), *Interactive learning: The art and science of teaching*. For a quick review of the lesson planning process see the checklist for writing lesson plans on p. 129. There are a number of lesson planning formats. You will need to use a lesson plan format approved by your instructor or supervisor. One lesson planning format which includes most of the categories in this curriculum guide can be found in Steinaker and Leavitt *Interactive learning: The art and science of teaching* (2008).

Writing Tips

When writing curriculum you use complete sentences in every component where writing is expected. Your introduction is one such component. Be sure that the narrative included in your written plan follows the APA format and style. Refer to the appropriate sections of this *Handbook* for specific directions on organization and writing. In some instances you check off or list teaching strategies used, SDAIE strategies used, specific assessment strategies, and in other categories as well. Write clearly and concisely. Use short simple statements because you may want to share this curriculum with your students. Several of the categories will only require one word or brief responses such as cognitive level, classroom materials, time and date of lesson, and technology. Your lesson plans should be easily understood both by those who review your plans and by your students with whom you use the plan. Make sure, in particular, that the sequence of each activity is clearly and concisely written. This component of the lesson plan is one of the keys to a successful lesson. It needs to be written clearly, specifically, and succinctly. Finally, make sure that your lesson plan, in all categories noted, is complete and can be clearly understood by reviewers and students.

20

End Note

Chapter

You have now completed a formal paper or project. This is one of several you will do in your graduate work and in your professional career. The exercise of formal writing is integral to your professional growth and to the development of your professional skills. As you grow professionally you will be expected to communicate your ideas, your perspectives, and your skills through writing as well as through speaking. Much of your written communication will be through formal writing. Formal writing skills help you in organizing, sequencing, interpreting information, drawing conclusions, and making recommendations. The utilization of these skills will be a strong asset in the development of your professionalism. Their use will also provide a basis for your growing perspectives and philosophy about your profession. Every strong leader needs to develop these qualities.

Be sure to keep your formal papers. A collection of these papers can be useful for reference and focus on issues, opportunities, and problems that may be a part of your professional assignment. The references you used for your papers can be a quick guide to obtaining sources and information. The bibliographies you have developed through your papers, particularly those with annotated bibliographies, can be a real asset to you professionally. Keep all of these. Wherever possible organize them topically so you can access sources on a particular issue. As part of your professional development, these papers, the references, and the bibliographies you have collected

> *Formal writing skills help you in organizing, sequencing, interpreting information, drawing conclusions, and making recommendations.*

can be very useful. Professionalism includes keeping current on issues and topics in the field. You should continue to read and reflect on these and add to your bibliography and sources as you continue your personal program of professional development. The acquisition of professional skills and experience can help you achieve you own personal professional goals. Congratulations on completing your paper and on your continuing development as a professional.

American Psychological Association. (2001). *Publication manual of the American Psychological Association* (5th ed.). Washington DC: Author.

Bennis, W. G. (1993). *An invented life: Reflections on leadership and change.* New York: Addison-Wesley.

Bennis, W. G. (2000). *Managing the dream.* Cambridge, MA Perseus Books Group.

Bennis, W., & Goldsmith, J. (2003). *Learning to lead* (3rd ed.). Cambridge, MA. Perseus Books Group.

Carver, R. P. (1984). *Writing a publishable research report in education, psychology, and related disciplines.* Springfield, IL: Charles C. Thomas.

Cone, J. D., & Foster, S. L. (1993). *Dissertations and theses from start to finish: Psychology and related fields.* Washington, DC: American Psychological Association.

Darling-Hammond, L (1997). *The right to learn: Blueprint for creating schools that work.* San Francisco, CA: Jossy-Bass Education Series.

Drucker, P. F. (1967). *The effective executive.* New York: Harper and Rowe.

Eisner, E. W. (1994). *The educational imagination on the design and evaluation of school programs.* (3rd ed.). New York: Macmillan College Publishing Company.

Gall, M. D., Borg, W. R., & Borg, J. P. (1996). *Educational research: An introduction* (6th ed.). White Plains, NY: Longman Publishers USA.

Howard, R. (Ed.). (1993). *The learning imperative: Managing people for continuous innovation.* Boston, MA: Harvard Business School.

Joyce, B., Weil, M., with Calhoun, E. (2004). *Models of teaching* (7th ed.). Needham Heights, MA: Allyn and Bacon.

Likert, R. (1967). *The human organization.* New York: McGraw Hill.

Merriam, S. B. (1998). *Qualitative research and case study applications in education* (2nd. ed.) San Francisco, CA: Jossey-Bass.

References

Mertens, D. M. (2004). *Research methods in education and psychology: Integrating diversity with quantitative and qualitative approaches* (2nd ed.). Thousand Oaks, CA: Sage Publishers.

Reeves, D. (2003). *Making standards work* (3rd ed.). Denver. CO: Center for Performance Assessment.

Sample, S. B. (2001). *The contrarian's guide to leadership.* San Francisco, CA: Jossey-Bass.

Serdyukov, P. & Ryan, M. (2008). *A five star approach to lesson planning.* Boston: Allyn and Bacon.

Steinaker, N. W. (2007). *Heuristic electronic lesson planner.* Trabuco Canyon, CA: Communications L. T. D. helplp.com

Steinaker, N. W., & Bell, M. R. (1979). *The experiential taxonomy: A new approach to teaching and learning.* New York: Academic Press

Steinaker, N. W. & Leavitt, L. S. (2008). *Interactive learning: The art and science of teaching.* Dubuque, IA: Kendall-Hunt Publishers.

Strunk, W. Jr., & White, E. B. (2000). *The elements of style* (4th ed.). New York: Allyn and Bacon.

Turabian, K. L. (1996). *A manual for writers of term papers, theses and dissertations* (6th ed.). Chicago, IL: University of Chicago Press.

Checklists for Sections of Formal Papers and Writing

A

In the pages that follows are a series of checklists. There is one for every section of the formal paper you are preparing. Also included are checklists for the table of contents, a bibliography, and appendixes. A generic checklist for conventions of formal writing in provided. Checklists for writing formal reports and white papers is included. In addition checklists for preparing a guidebook or handbook, staff development programs, grant proposals, action research studies and preparing curriculum are included The checklist for formal writing should be used as the final check of your paper. Each checklist is designed for your personal review of the paper you have prepared as the writer. You can use these checklists both as you write and as a final review to determine if you have completed all the necessary components of each section of your paper or study. This is done to ensure that you have followed the formal writing conventions as well as the APA format and expected components of each section of the paper.

In addition, if you are a student writer, there is a signature form for you and for your instructor including the date when the checklist is completed and provided for the instructor. These checklists can also be used for conferences between you and your instructor or supervisor. Space is provided on each of the checklists for comments by you, by your instructor or by your supervisor. Page numbers referents are included to note the page number in the *Handbook* where the information needed to complete the each point on the checklist is provided. During the preparation of your paper, you may need to use several of the checklists more than once when you conference with your instructor or supervisor. If you are enrolled in a class, these checklists may be provided for you by your instructor. They can also be obtained through the publisher.

If you are writing your paper individually for submission to a specific audience or to a journal or other publication, these checklists are provided to ensure that you have followed the format suggested within the *Handbook* and are consistent with the APA. Be sure to use them because they provide you with a final check about your adherence to formal writing conventions and to the format outlined in the *Handbook*. Again, our best wishes to you as you use these checklists. We are sure that you will find them helpful. If you need additional copies of the checklists or the *Handbook*, please ask your instructor or your supervisor for copies. You may also contact the publisher.

Checklist for Preparing the Title Page

Directions: Please fill out the checklist below. Circle yes or no for each item listed. Make any comments necessary in the space provided. Page numbers following each item indicate the references to the page or pages where you will find the information about how to complete the item.

1. I have included a page header (3) . . . . Yes   No

2. I have included a running head (3) . . . . Yes   No

3. I have provided the full title of my paper (4) . . . . Yes   No

4. My (our) name (s) as author (s) is listed below the title (4) . . . . Yes   No

5. I have included the author's affiliation (4) . . . . Yes   No

6. I have provided any other information expected by the instructor, the organization, or the group to which the paper will be submitted. (3–4) . . . . Yes   No

7. All elements of the title page are centered as specified and are in place (3–4) . . . . Yes   No

Comments:

_____

_____

_____

_____

Writers Signature _____

Instructors Signature _____ Date _____

Checklist for Table of Contents

Directions: Please fill out the checklist below. Circle yes or no for each item listed. Make any comments necessary in the space provided. Page numbers following each item reference the page or pages on which you will find information necessary to complete the item.

1. Table of contents has a page header numbered in lower case Roman numerals (6) .... Yes   No

2. The table of contents immediately follows the title page (6) .... Yes   No

3. Ellipses are correctly entered (6) .... Yes   No

4. Section headings or chapter numbers are justified to the left margin (6) .... Yes   No

5. Categories are indented one tab space (6) .... Yes   No

6. Subcategories are indented two tab spaces (6) .... Yes   No

7. Page numbers are justified to the right margin (6) .... Yes   No

8. Appendixes are listed by title and page number in the table of contents (6) .... Yes   No

Comments:

_____

_____

_____

_____

Writers Signature _____

Instructors Signature _____ Date _____

Checklist for Preparing the Abstract

Directions: Please fill out the checklist below. Circle yes or no for each item listed. Make any comments necessary in the space provided. Page numbers following each item indicate the reference to the page or pages where you will find the information on how to complete the item.

1. I have included a page header numbered two (3) . . . .   Yes   No

2. The word abstract appears as the title one double space
   below page header (8) . . . .   Yes   No

3. My abstract is blocked (8) . . . .   Yes   No

4. My abstract contains no more than 120 words (150 if
   approved by instructor) (8) . . . .   Yes   No

5. My abstract is accurate, concise, and specific (9) . . . .   Yes   No

6. I have included salient points from the review of literature (9) . . . . .   Yes   No

7. The abstract was written in the past tense (9) . . . .   Yes   No

8. I have included results of my research study (9) . . . .   Yes   No

9. I have included conclusions and recommendations (9) . . . .   Yes   No

10. I wrote my abstract after the other sections of the paper were
    completed (9) . . . .   Yes   No

11. No personal bias or opinion is included within the abstract (9) . . . .   Yes   No

Comments:

_____

_____

_____

_____

Writers Signature _____

Instructors Signature _____   Date _____

Checklist for Preparing the Introduction

Directions: Please fill out the form below. Circle yes or no for each item listed. Make any comments necessary in the space provided. Page numbers following each item indicate the reference to the page or pages where you will find information on how to complete the item.

1. I have included a page header numbered three (3) . . . . Yes   No

2. Full title of paper is given one double space below the
   page header (11) . . . . Yes   No

3. The purpose of the paper is clearly stated at the beginning
   of the paper (11) . . . . Yes   No

4. The purpose includes limitations of the topic, the area of study,
   questions or issues, and other information especially if you are
   writing a research study (11–12) . . . . Yes   No

5. The importance of the paper/study has been evidenced with
   citations (12) . . . . Yes   No

6. Works cited reflected the author's feeling about importance
   of the topic (12–13) . . . . Yes   No

7. I have prepared my rationale for choosing the topic (13) . . . . Yes   No

8. Everything in the introduction except from direct quotes was
   written in the past or present perfect tense (13) . . . . Yes   No

Comments:

_____

_____

_____

_____

Writers Signature _____

Instructors Signature _____ Date _____

Checklist for Preparing the Review of Literature

Directions: Please fill out the checklist below. Circle yes or no for each item listed. Make any comments necessary in the space provided. Page numbers following each item indicate the reference to the page or pages where you will find the information on how to complete the item.

1. I have included a page header on every page of the review of literature (3) . . . . Yes   No

2. Review begins with an opening paragraph listing categories and subcategories (15) . . . . Yes   No

3. The categories are on a separate line from text and are italicized (16) . . . Yes   No

4. I have used at least two categories and at least two subcategories where needed (16) . . . . Yes   No

5. I have used no personal commentary in any part of the review of literature (16) . . . . Yes   No

6. Subcategory names are indented, italicized, followed by a period on a text line (18) . . . . Yes   No

7. I have cited sources for every new idea or information I have introduced (17) . . . . Yes   No

8. Everything is written in past or present perfect tense except in direct quotes (17) . . . . Yes   No

9. I have put quotation marks around each quote under forty words along with citation and page number (17) . . . . Yes   No

10. I have blocked quotes of forty or more words using no quotation marks (17) . . . . Yes   No

11. I have cited every quote of forty or more words and included page number (17) . . . . Yes   No

12. Everything in the review of literature is double spaced.(20) . . . . Yes   No

13. I have provided an evidentiary base for my conclusions and
recommendations (20). . . . . Yes   No

14. If needed, I have included a closing paragraph (18) . . . . Yes   No

Comments:

_____

_____

_____

_____

Writers Signature _____

Instructors Signature _____ Date _____

Checklist for Preparing the Method Section

Directions: Please fill out the checklist given below. Circle yes or no for each item listed. Make any comments in the space provided. Page numbers following the item are the reference page or pages where you will find information about how to complete the item.

1. I have included a page header for each page (3) . . . . Yes   No

2. I have made each of the topics listed as a separate category (21) . . . . Yes   No

3. I have completed the question or issue section (21–22) . . . . Yes   No

4. I have used the past tense or present perfect tense throughout
   this section (28) . . . . Yes   No

5. I have noted limitations, variables, population and sampling
   process (22–25) . . . . Yes   No

6. I have discussed the time frame and process (25–26) . . . . Yes   No

7. I have addressed data collection, data analysis, assessment
   and evaluation (26–28) . . . . Yes   No

8. I have selected the data analysis mode, either qualitative
   or quantitative (27–28) . . . . Yes   No

9. I have provided enough detail in each section for clarity
   and understanding (28) . . . . Yes   No

Comments:

_____

_____

_____

_____

Writers Signature _____

Instructors Signature _____ Date _____

Checklist for Preparing the Results Section

Directions: Please fill out the checklist given below. Circle yes or no for each item listed. Make any comments in the space provided. Numbers following each item are references to the pages in the *Handbook* where you can find information about how to complete each item.

1. I have included a page header on each page of this section (3) . . . . . Yes No

2. I have obtained results in a quantitative study using descriptive statistics, inferential statistics, or correlational statistical analysis (30–31)* . . . . Yes No

3. I have obtained results in a qualitative study with personal interpretation (33–34)*. . . . . Yes No

4. I have presented my results in a clear and concise way (30–32) . . . . . Yes No

5. I have included figures or tables, as needed, to present and clarify results (30) . . . . Yes No

6. I have written my results section in past or present perfect tense (34) . . . . Yes No

7. The results are clearly and cogently written (31–34) . . . . Yes No

8. There is no bias, interpretation, or personal perspective in this section (30) . . . . Yes No

9. I have disaggregated the data, as necessary, for each variable in the results (32) . . . . Yes No

* Select only one.

Comments:

_____

_____

_____

_____

Writers Signature _____

Instructors Signature _____ Date _____

Checklist for Review of Literature Paper Discussion Section

Directions: Please fill out the checklist given below. Circle yes or no for each item listed. Make any comments in the space provided. Numbers following each item indicate the page numbers in the *Handbook* on which you can find information about how to complete the item.

1. I have included a page header for each page in this section (3) . . . . . Yes   No

2. I have included a summary of the review of literature written
   in past or present perfect tense (38) . . . . Yes   No

3. I have used citations in the summary (38) . . . . Yes   No

4. I have interpreted the literature carefully and clearly using
   present tense and the personal pronoun I (38–39) . . . . Yes   No

5. I have provided an evidentiary base for my conclusions (37–38) . . . Yes   No

6. My conclusions are clearly and succinctly stated (39) . . . . Yes   No

7. Recommendations are based on evidence, the conclusions,
   and are clearly stated (39) . . . . Yes   No

8. I have expressed my personal views on the review of literature
   in the interpretation, the conclusions, and the
   recommendations. (38–39) . . . . Yes   No

9. I did not elaborate or go into detail in my conclusions and
   recommendations (39) . . . . Yes   No

Comments:

_____

_____

_____

_____

Writers Signature _____

Instructors Signature _____ Date _____

Checklist for Discussion Section of Research Studies

Directions: Please respond to each item listed below. Circle yes or no for each item. Make any comments in the space provided. Numbers following the item are the reference pages in the *Handbook* on which you can find information about how to complete the item.

1. I have summarized my results and related them to the review of literature (40–41) .... Yes   No

2. I have cited studies related to this topic in the summary (40–41) ... Yes   No

3. Results of this study have been related to other research studies (40–41) .... Yes   No

4. I have presented my views of results in the interpretation section (41–42) .... Yes   No

5. I have interpreted the review of literature in terms of the results and the content of the review of literature (41–42) .... Yes   No

6. The review of literature provided an evidentiary base for the study (42) .... Yes   No

7. Conclusions were clear and concise and were drawn from the review of literature and the results (42–43) .... Yes   No

8. Recommendations were clear and concise and drawn from the review of literature and the results (43) .... Yes   No

Comments:

_____

_____

_____

_____

Writers Signature _____

Instructors Signature _____ Date _____

Checklist for Reference Section

Directions: Please respond to each item listed below. Circle yes or no for each item. Make comments in the space provided. Numbers following each item refer to pages in the *Handbook* where you can find information on how to complete the item.

1. References follow the APA style (48) .... Yes   No

2. References are alphabetized by author or title when no author is listed (48) .... Yes   No

3. Internet pathways are listed without underlining and in black with an APA approved 12 point typeface (48) .... Yes   No

4. Everything in the reference section is double spaced (48) .... Yes   No

5. I have listed only the sources cited in the body of the paper (48) ... Yes   No

6. References are hanging reference with succeeding lines indented one tab space (48) .... Yes   No

Comments:

_____

_____

_____

_____

Writers Signature _____

Instructors Signature _____ Date _____

Checklist for Formal Writing

Directions: Please fill out the form below. Circle yes or no for each item listed. Make any comments necessary in the space provided. Page numbers following each item indicate the reference to the page or pages in the *Handbook* where you will find the information about how to complete the item.

1. There are no agreement errors in my paper (51) .... Yes No

2. I have eliminated all anthropomorphisms from my paper (52) ..... Yes No

3. My citations follow the APA style (52–53) .... Yes No

4. I have eliminated colloquialisms, idioms, and slang expressions from my paper (53) .... Yes No

5. My ellipses follow *Handbook* guidelines (53) .... Yes No

6. I have not ended or begun any line in my paper with a hyphen (53) ... Yes No

7. My paper is justified only on the left margin except for page headers (54) .... Yes No

8. I have used specific and precise language in my paper (54) .... Yes No

9. I have eliminated most or all of the he/shes from my paper (51) .... Yes No

10. I have no comma splices, run on sentences, or fragments in my paper (56–57) .... Yes No

11. I have used that and who correctly (57) .... Yes No

12. I have used the appropriate tenses in all sections of my paper (57) .... Yes No

13. There is no plagiarism in my paper (55) .... Yes No

Comments:

_____

_____

_____

_____

Writers Signature _____

Instructors Signature _____ Date _____

Checklist for Appendixes

Appendixes may not be needed, nor required for your paper or study. If they are, please fill out the checklist below.

Directions: Please fill out the form below. Circle yes or no for each item listed. Make any comments in the space provided. Page numbers following each items are referents for the page or pages on which you will find information needed to complete the item.

1. I have included a page header (3) . . . .   Yes   No

2. My appendixes follow the references and the bibliography
   (if included) (50) . . . .   Yes   No

3. Each appendix has a title (50) . . . .   Yes   No

4. If more than one appendix is included it is lettered A, B, C, D
   and so forth (50) . . . .   Yes   No

5. My appendixes include information pertinent to my paper or
   study (50) . . . .   Yes   No

6. My appendixes are listed in the table of contents (50) . . . .   Yes   No

7. I have referred to the appendixes in the appropriate sections of
   my paper (50) . . . .   Yes   No

8. I have followed APA style and format for all appendixes (50) . . . . . .   Yes   No

Comments:

_____

_____

_____

_____

Writers Signature _____

Instructors Signature _____ Date _____

Checklist for Bibliography

A bibliography is not always required in a review of literature or a research study. If it is required, please complete this checklist.

Directions: Please fill out the form below. Circle yes or no for each item listed. Make any comments in the space provided. Page numbers following each item are referents for the page or pages on which you will find information needed to complete the item.

1. I have included a page header for the bibliography (3) . . . . Yes   No

2. My bibliography immediately follows the references and is on a separate page (50) . . . . Yes   No

3. My bibliography contains only additional resources directly related to my topic(50) . . . . Yes   No

4. I have annotated each entry in the bibliography (50) . . . . Yes   No

5. My annotations are blocked and begin one double space below the entry (50) . . . . Yes   No

6. I have followed APA for each entry into the bibliography (50) . . . . . Yes   No

7. Entries are listed by author or title where no author is given (50) . . . Yes   No

8. I have not included entries unrelated to the topic of my paper (50) . . . . Yes   No

Comments:

_____

_____

_____

_____

Writers Signature _____

Instructors Signature _____ Date _____

Checklist for Formal Report or White Paper

Directions: Please fill out the checklist below. Circle yes or no for each item listed. Make any comments necessary in the space provided. Page numbers following each item indicate the reference to the page or pages where you will find information on how to complete the item.

1. I have identified the purpose of the report or paper (66) . . . .   Yes   No

2. I have followed the conventions of formal writing (59–65) . . . .   Yes   No

3. I have provided an introduction (66–67.) . . . .   Yes   No

4. I have included citations of source material (66–67) . . . .   Yes   No

5. I have included background information for the readers (67–68) . . .   Yes   No

6. I have discussed how the issue was dealt with historically and
   in other venues (68) . . . .   Yes   No

7. I have used mostly simple declarative sentences and an economy
   of expression (60) . . . .   Yes   No

8. I have presented conclusions and recommendations (67) . . . .   Yes   No

9. I have included a reference section (48–49) . . . .   Yes   No

Comments:

_____

_____

_____

_____

Writers Signature _____

Instructors Signature _____   Date _____

Checklist for a Guidebook or Handbook

Directions: Please fill out the checklist below. Circle yes or no for each item listed. Make any comments necessary in the space provided. Page numbers following each item indicate the reference to the page or pages where you will find information on how to complete the item.

1. I have provided an introduction (71) . . . .   Yes   No

2. I have included backup information in appendixes (71) . . . .   Yes   No

3. I have explained each step clearly and concisely (71) . . . .   Yes   No

4. I have sequenced each step in the process with economy of
   expressional (71) . . . .   Yes   No

5. I have used simple declarative sentences and have avoided
   technical language (71) . . . .   Yes   No

6. I have followed the conventions of formal writing (59–65) . . . .   Yes   No

7. I have included a reference section (71) . . . .   Yes   No

8. I have included a table of contents (71) . . . .   Yes   No

Comments:

_____

_____

_____

_____

Writers Signature _____

Instructors Signature _____ Date _____

Checklist for Staff Development Programs

Directions: Please fill out the checklist below. Circle yes or no for each item listed. Make any comments necessary in the space provided. Page numbers following each item indicate the reference to the page or pages where you will find information on how to complete the item.

1. I have developed a needs assessment and included it in an
   appendix (73) . . . . Yes   No

2. I have identified expected outcomes of the program (74) . . . . Yes   No

3. I have identified personnel needs and job descriptions (75–76) . . . . Yes   No

4. I have developed an organizational plan for the program (76) . . . . . Yes   No

5. I have identified workshop presenters and workshop leaders
   (76–77) . . . . Yes   No

6. I have defined the role of the evaluator (76–77) . . . . Yes   No

7. I have included resource needs for the program (77) . . . . Yes   No

8. I have a plan to meet the differentiated needs of participants
   (77–78) . . . . Yes   No

9. I have included strategies for involving participants (78) . . . . Yes   No

10. I have developed an evaluation plan (78–79) . . . . Yes   No

Comments:

_____

_____

_____

_____

Writers Signature _____

Instructors Signature _____ Date _____

Checklist for Preparing Program Evaluations

Directions: Please fill out the checklist below. Circle yes or no for each item listed. Make any comments necessary in the space provided. Page numbers following each item indicate the reference to the page or pages where you will find information on how to complete the item.

1. I have included background information on the program (79–80) . . . . Yes   No

2. I have included a timeline and schedule of activities (80) . . . . Yes   No

3. I have questions for interviews with managers, personnel, and stakeholders (81) . . . . Yes   No

4. I have a schedule for observations and noted what needs to be observed (81) . . . . Yes   No

5. I have prepared a final report including program strengths and limitations (81–82) . . . . Yes   No

6. I have included a narrative of what was learned including recommendations (81–82) . . . . Yes   No

7. I have included citations and a reference section in the report (82) . . . . Yes   No

8. I have outlined the agenda and process of the final open report (82) . . . . Yes   No

9. I have followed the conventions of formal writing (59–65) . . . . Yes   No

Comments:

_____

_____

_____

_____

Writers Signature _____

Instructors Signature _____   Date _____

Checklist for Grant Proposals

Directions: Please fill out the checklist below. Circle yes or no for each item listed. Make any comments necessary in the space provided. Page numbers following each item indicate the reference to the page or pages where you will find information on how to complete the item.

1. I have followed the guidelines of the RFP (84) .... Yes   No

2. I have specifically identified the problem/issue being addressed (84) ... Yes   No

3. I have defined the interventions clearly and concisely (84) .... Yes   No

4. I have developed goals and specific objectives for the program (84) .... Yes   No

5. I have described a sequence of activities to achieve the goals and objectives (84) .... Yes   No

6. Benchmarks and expected outcomes have been developed (84) .... Yes   No

7. I have noted the evaluation strategies/protocols to be used (84) .... Yes   No

8. I have prepared a budget with seven categories (85) .... Yes   No

9. I have identified personnel needed for the program (85) .... Yes   No

10. I have identified personnel roles within the program (85) .... Yes   No

11. Stakeholders have been noted including non program personnel (85) .. Yes   No

12. I have addressed compliance issues (85) .... Yes   No

13. I have included demographic data (85) .... Yes   No

14. I have followed the conventions of formal writing (59–65) .... Yes   No

Comments:

_____

_____

_____

_____

Writers Signature _____

Instructors Signature _____   Date _____

Checklist for Action Research

Directions: Please fill out the checklist below. Circle yes or no for each item listed. Make any comments necessary in the space provided. Page numbers following each item indicate the reference to the page or pages where you will find information on how to complete the item.

1. I have clearly stated the purpose of the action research (87) .... Yes   No

2. I have identified specific objectives for the action research (87–88) .... Yes   No

3. I have established a rationale for the action research (88) .... Yes   No

4. I have cited sources and included a reference page (88) .... Yes   No

5. I have defined the intervention or interventions clearly and concisely (88) .... Yes   No

6. The process of implementation has been sequentially presented (88–89) .... Yes   No

7. I have included a timeline of the components of the interventions (89) .... Yes   No

8. I have developed a well defined evaluation design (89) .... Yes   No

9. I have prepared conclusions and recommendations (89–90) .... Yes   No

10. I have followed the conventions of formal writing (59–65) .... Yes   No

Comments:

_____

_____

_____

_____

Writers Signature _____

Instructors Signature _____ Date _____

Checklist for Developing Curriculum

Directions: Please fill out the checklist given below. Circle yes or no for each item listed. Make any comments in the space provided. Page numbers following the item are the reference or pages to the pages where you will find information about how to complete the item.

1. I have completed the introduction (97) .... Yes   No

2. My lessons are linked together in a unit, theme, or area of focus (97) ... Yes   No

3. Identified state (or district) standards are included (97–98) .... Yes   No

4. Long range objectives (outcomes) are included for the lesson
   sequence (98–99) .... Yes   No

5. An objective (s) is included for each individual lesson (98–99) ..... Yes   No

6. A time frame is included for lesson or lessons (99) .... Yes   No

7. Classroom structures and program materials are included (99–101) ... Yes   No

8. Technology used for each lesson is included (101) .... Yes   No

9. Cognitive level expected to be achieved for each lesson is
   included (101–102) .... Yes   No

10. Teaching strategies for each lesson are included (102–105) .... Yes   No

11. SDAIE strategies are listed for each lesson (105–107) .... Yes   No

11. Assessment strategies for each lesson are included (107) .... Yes   No

12. Instructional processes for each lesson is included (107–108) ...... Yes   No

13. A reflection on the lesson is included (108) .... Yes   No

14. I have used APA format and style for narrative sections (pp. 51–57) ... Yes   No

15. I have used an instructor approved format for lessons (108–109) .... Yes   No

Comments:

_____

_____

_____

_____

Writers Signature _____

Instructors Signature _____   Date _____

B Suggested Scoring Rubrics

Below is a suggested scoring rubric for review of literature papers and research papers. You may make any adjustments needed for your class or for your course. The first scoring rubric is for review of literature papers, the second is for research studies. These rubrics are based on a hundred point scale.

Review of Literature Papers

Adherence to APA style as noted in the *Handbook* 15

Follows conventions of formal writing and writing tips
in the *Handbook* 10

Content of the introduction 5

Content of the review of literature 55

Content of the discussion 10

References 5

Research Studies

Adherence to APA style as noted in the *Handbook* 15

Follows conventions of formal writing and writing tips
in the *Handbook* 10

Content of introduction 10

Content of review of literature 15

C   Suggested Evaluation Guide

Below are suggested evaluation deductions from papers. You can use this or one of your own construction. Any changes you wish to make can be used for your class. The numbers indicate the suggested loss of points. If the number is two or more you can deduct up to that number.

1. Major syntax error (comma fault, run on, fragment) 3
2. Failure to follow APA format as found in *Handbook* 5
3. More than three agreement errors 1
4. Organization of paper 4
5. Reference errors 1
6. Errors in citations 1
7. Errors in quotations (block quotations, direct quotes,
   page numbers) 1
8. Errors in tense (consistent use of wrong tense) 3
9. Referent errors 1
10. Spacing errors (everything is double spaced) 2
11. Errors in table of contents (where required) 1
12. Errors in abstract (number of words, not blocked,
    missing some elements) 1
13. Word choice (use precise word) 1
14. Sentences (mostly simple sentences; some compound or
    complex sentences) 2

15. Use of superscript or subscript except in certain mathematics or
    science formulae 1
16. Errors in ellipses 1
17. Other errors (to be determined by instructor) 2

Format for Presentation of Paper

This format is designed for oral presentations. Power Point presentations can be used in conjunction with oral presentations. Other media may also be used. Organization is key to a strong presentation. As Pope noted "brevity is the soul of wit." Do not be loquacious or verbose. As we have already stated, verbosity is the last refuge of mediocrity. We have keyed this presentation format to a brief presentation of five to eight minutes with two minutes for questions and comments. Longer presentations can go into greater detail and more specificity. They will take more time, but should follow the same format presented below. The presentation format is consistent with the organization of the paper.

Review of Literature Paper

1. State the purpose of your paper.
2. Establish the importance of the topic. This can be done in one or two sentences.
3. Note why you chose this topic.
4. Identify the categories and subcategories of the review of literature.
5. Highlight one or two salient points from each category.
6. In the discussion summarize your review of literature.
7. In the discussion Interpret your review of literature.
8. Cite your conclusions.
9. Make your recommendations

This is all you do for a review of literature paper. For brief presentations, this kind of oral presentation can be done in five minutes or less. Longer presentations, if agreed upon by the instructor or supervisor, can be made.

Research Studies

1. State the purpose of your study. Include information about area of study, limitations, variables, and other pertinent information. State these briefly.
2. Establish the importance of your topic. Use citations as needed.
3. Tell why you selected the topic
4. Name the categories and subcategories of the review of literature.
5. Identify salient points from the review of literature including other studies about the topic.
6. For the method section restate the purpose of the study, mention time frame, limitations, population, sampling, process, data collection, data analysis, and assessment and evaluation. Do this briefly and avoid any redundancies. Sometimes you can bring two or more categories of the method section together. Tailor the details to the allotted time frame for presentation.
7. Present the results section by noting the variables tested, the and the statistical measures used for analysis.
8. Provide result for each variable keyed to statements on surveys, questionnaires, and interviews.
9. Note the ones on which you are reporting and give results for each.
10. Inferential and correlational statistical analyses require statements of significance.
11. Note any comments from surveys or questionnaires
12. Establish the meaning of the results in a summative statement.
13. Summarize the review of literature and emphasize how it related to your study.
14. Correlate your findings with the review of literature.
15. Interpret the meaning of your findings including interpretation of the literature reviewed.
16. State your conclusions.
17. State your recommendations.

With careful organization and the presentation of only the most important information, a brief report of this kind can be completed in five to eight minutes with a few minutes for questions an comments following. Any presentation should be tightly organized, succinctly presented, as well as being clear and cogent to the audience. Longer presentations can, of course be allowed by the instructor or supervisor. Best wishes to you on your presentation.

E

Sample References

Below are listed some references most of which are taken directly from the APA manual. Review these and if you have additional questions, please ask your instructor or supervisor or refer directly to the APA manual.

Book, two authors

Steinaker, N. W., & Bell, M. R. (1979). *The experiential taxonomy: A new approach to teaching and learning.* New York: Academic Press.

Journal article, three to six authors

Saywitz, K. J., Mannarino, A. P., Berliner, L., & Cohen, J. A. (2000). Treatment for sexually abused children and adolescents. *American Psychologist*, 55, 1040–1049.

Magazine article

Kandel, E. R., & Squire, L. R. (2000, November 10), Neuroscience: Breaking down scientific barriers to the study of brain and mind. *Science*, 290, 1112–1120.

Daily newspaper article, no author

New drug appears to sharply cut risk of death from heart failure. (1993, July 15). *The Washington Post*, p. A12.

Abstract as original source

Wood, N. J., Young, S. L., Fanselow, M. S., & Butcher, L. L. (1991). MAP-2 expression in cholinoceptive pyramidal cells or rodent cortex and hippocampus is altered by Pavlovian conditioning [abstract]. *Society for Neuroscience Abstracts.* 17, 480.

Book, third edition, Jr. in name

Mitchell, T. R., & Larson, J. R., Jr. (1987). *People in organizations: An introduction to organizational behavior* (3rd ed.). New York: McGraw-Hill.

Edited book

Gibbs, J. T., & Huang, L. N. (Eds.), (1991). *Children of color: Psychological interventions with minority youth.* San Francisco: Jossey-Bass.

Article or chapter from an edited book, two editors

Bjork, R. A. (1989). Retrieval inhibition as an adaptive mechanism in human memory. In H. L. Roediger II & F. I. M. Craik (Eds.), *Varieties of memory & consciousness* (pp. 309–330). Hillsdale, NJ: Erlbaum.

Entry in an encyclopedia

Bergmann, P. G. (1993). Relativity. In *The new encyclopaedia Britannica* (Vol. 26, pp. 501–558). Chicago: Encyclopedia Britannica.

Note: When the article has no author listed, place the title in the author position.

Report available from ERIC

Mead, J. V. (1992). *Looking at old photographs: Investigating the teacher tales that novice teachers bring with them* (Report No. NCRTL-RR-9204). East Lansing, MI: National Center for Research on Teacher Learning. (ERIC Document Reproduction Service No. ED346082).

Published proceedings of meetings or symposia

Deci, E. L., & Ryan, R. M. (1991). A motivational approach to self: Integration in personality. In R. Dienstbier (Ed.). *Nebraska Symposium on Motivation:* Vol. 38. *Perspectives on motivation* (pp. 237–288). Lincoln: University of Nebraska Press.

Doctoral dissertations and master's theses abstracted in **Dissertation Abstracts International** *from the University of Michigan*

Brower, D. L. (1993). Employee assistant programs supervisory referrals: Characteristics of referring and nonreferring supervisors. *Dissertation Abstracts International,* 54 (01), 534B. (UMI No. 9315947)

Unpublished manuscript not submitted for publication

Stinson, C., Milbrath, C, Reidbord, S. & Bucci, W. (1992). *Thematic segmentation of psychotherapy transcripts for convergent analyses.* Unpublished manuscript.

Manuscript in progress or submitted for publication but not yet accepted

Steinaker, N. W., Mbuva, J, & Holm, M. (2005). *A taxonomy of motivation: From theory to practice.* Manuscript submitted for publication.

Internet articles based on a print source

VandenBos, G., Knapp, S., & Doe, J. (2001). Role of reference elements in the selection of resources by psychology undergraduates [Electronic version], *Journal of Bibliographic Research, 5,* 117–123.

Stand-alone internet document, no author identified, no date

GVU's 8th WWW user survey. (n.d.). Retrieved August 8, 2000, from http://www.cc.gatech.edu/gvu/user_surveys/survey-1997-10/

Message posted to a newsgroup

Chalmers, D. (2000, November 17). Seeing with sound [Msg 1]. Message posted to news://sci.psychology.consciousness

Electronic copy of a journal article, retrieved from database

Borman, W. C., Hanson, M. A., Oppler, S. H., Pulakos, E. D., & White, L. A. (1993). Role of early supervisor performance. *Journal of Applied Psychology, 78,* 443–449. Retrieved October 23, 2000, from PsychARTICLES database.

F Preparing Surveys and Questionnaires

Often in preparation for a research study you need to prepare a survey or a questionnaire. Both need to begin with a strong focus on the purpose of your study. Develop a simple and direct set of directions for filling out the survey or questionnaire. Start your survey or questionnaire with demographic questions about the population you are asking to respond to your survey or your questionnaire. Demographic information includes such elements as age, gender, work assignment, ethnicity, area of residence, and other descriptive demographic information. Demographic information is important because from this information you may identify some or all of the variables you wish to test.

Next you develop statements or questions to gather responses from your population. Determine the most important information you want to obtain and include those statements or questions early in the survey or questionnaire. Make statements or ask questions that are clearly written and can be easily understood by your population. Avoid value words wherever possible and avoid words that can be interpreted in more than one way. Make your statements and questions specific, to the point, and limited to identified information you wish to obtain. Make sure that each question or statement addresses only one issue or area about which to respond. In a survey make space available to comments by respondents. If you wish to have them respond to a specific statement, make space available after that statement. You may also make space available at the end of the survey. In a questionnaire establish some limits to your questions. You may want to ask your respondents to use only the space provided. You may also want to get as much information as possible, so invite them to extend their responses if they wish.

If you are using a survey, you may use a Likert Scale which has strongly agree, agree, disagree, strongly disagree possible responses. You may use a numeric scale and ask your population to circle the number that describes their response. Make sure you identify what each number means. You may also use a semantic differential scale if you wish. There are a variety of formats for your survey. Select the one that best fits the population you are studying.

You may also use any of these formats for a questionnaire if you wish. Many questionnaires are set up so that respondents can make comments. In a survey or questionnaire you can tally your responses and then use statistical measures to analyze, assess, and interpret data from the survey or questionnaire. You can summarize or categorize the comments. You may also wish to identify the responses anonymously through the demographic data you have collected. Make sure as you develop your instrument that it can serve to elicit responses that will help you gather the data you need to find results that focus on the major purpose of your study.

G Elements of Formal Grammar Usage

It is very important that you become familiar with the grammatical expectations for formal writing and use them consistently. We have discussed many of these expectations in the writing tips which follow section. A number of these expectations are also found in the common errors section and in the section on conventions of formal writing. We felt however, there was a need to bring together information about grammar in a section of this work where it would be easily accessible to you, the writer. While we have included many grammatical expectations, there are others about which you need to be aware. The content of this appendix is designed as a quick reference to help you clarify identified grammar issues related to formal writing. It is not as a complete guide to grammar. You should have available a more complete guide when you are writing. There are many resources you can use. Among them Turabian (1996), Strunk and White (2000), and the *Manual* of the APA. This section on grammar is divided into three categories: Punctuation, syntax, and other grammar expectations. This information is organized alphabetically by category for easy use. Refer to it as needed when you are preparing your papers.

Punctuation

Abbreviations: Abbreviations are seldom used in formal writing. Generally the whole word is written and abbreviations are not used. Some forms of address such as Mr., Mrs., Ms., and Dr. may be used. Abbreviations like Sr., Jr., III, and IV (senior, junior, third, and fourth) may be included in a formal paper. Certain abbreviations for scholarly degrees and titles of respect following full names are set off by two commas when used in text. State names can be given their two letter abbreviations. You may abbreviate such terms as avenue, boulevard, street, and directions (N, S, E, W). Abbreviations are followed by a period.

Active voice: The active voice is more direct than the passive voice. The active voice in writing is more concise and more definite.

Active voice: *I will always remember my first visit to Denver.*

Passive voice: *My first visit to Denver will always be remembered by me.*

Acronyms: A series of letters or a word formed from the initial letter of each of the successive parts of a compound term. For example: *Heuristic Electronic Lesson Planner* (HELP). Note that after the first use of the compound term, the acronym is used in parantheses. In successive usages the acronym may be used in place of the compound term without parantheses.

Anthropomorphism: Attributing human characteristics to animals or inanimate sources. For example: *Research said. The school program was persuaded. . . .*

Brackets: Brackets [ ] are primarily used for insertions into quoted matter for editorial comments, corrections, and clarifications inserted into quoted matter.

Capitalization: A capital letter is used in the first letter of proper nouns (names of persons, places, and specific things). Proper nouns that have lost their original meaning and have become part of general language use are not capitalized. An example is roman numerals. The first letter of the first word of a sentence is capitalized. In titles of books and articles in reference lists, capitalize only the first word. Also capitalize the first word after a colon or dash. Capitalize trade and brand names of drugs, equipment, and foods.

Colons: The colon is used to introduce a clause or a phrase that expands, clarifies, or exemplifies the meaning of what precedes it. In formal writing the first word following a colon is capitalized. A colon is used between chapter and verse in referring to scripture.

Commas: Commas are used more frequently in formal writing than in other writing styles. Commas are used to separate a series of three or more items in a list. They are used after yes and no. They are used between appositives, following an adverbial beginning of a sentence, and following author's names in a reference section. Enclose parenthetic expression in sentences with commas. Commas follow abbreviations of academic degrees and titles. Place a comma before a conjunction introducing an independent clause. A comma follows words such as *namely, that is, nevertheless,* and *for example.* When a long prepositional phrase introduces a sentence, it is followed by a comma. A comma is used to separate main clauses joined by a coordinating conjunction such as *and, but, or, nor,* or *so.* A comma is used with compound predicates. Commas are used to set off transitional words or phrases such as *indeed.*

Dashes: Dashes are seldom used in formal writing. In a few instances a dash can be used to introduce an element that emphasizes or explains the main clause through of one or more key words.

Hyphens: When two or more words are combined to form a compound adjective, a hyphen can be used. Do not begin a line or end a line with a hyphen. Prefixes such as *mid, multi,* and *non* do not require hyphens.

Italics: You use italics for for titles of books, periodicals, and microfilm publications. Italicize letters that are used as test scores or scales: A *t* test or the *n* was thirty.

Parantheses: Parantheses are principally used in the text to set off parenthetical elements and to enclose the source of a quotation or a paraphrase. A citation is enclosed by parantheses.

Passive voice: A verb form indicating that the subject is being acted on. The passive voice is acceptable in expository writing, but is less used in formal writing.

Periods: A period ends a sentence or a sentence that is neither a question nor an exclamation. A period punctuates some abbreviations. Periods are used with a person's initials followed by a space. A period follows numerals and letters in an outline.

Quotation Marks: Quotation marks enclose direct quotations but not indirect quotations or paraphrases. Quotation marks enclose fragments of quoted material. Quotation marks are not included in blocked quotes of more than forty words.

Semicolons: A semicolon should be used between the parts of a compound sentence of two or more independent clauses when not connected by a conjunction. If clauses of a compound sentence are long and have commas within them, they should be separated by a semicolon. If the second cause is preceded by an adverb such as *accordingly, besides, then, therefore,* or *thus,* and not by a conjunction, the semicolon is required.

Titles of tests: Titles of tests are capitalized except for articles and prepositions. Do not capitalize the generic titles of test such as a *normative test* or a *standardized test.* Do not capitalize words such as *test* or *scale* if they refer to subscales of tests.

Syntax

Abruptness: A series of short sentences can cause choppiness or abruptness in sentences. Varied sentence lengths are more appropriate. Direct declarative sentences in the active voice with simple, common words are usually best. Read your paper aloud to ensure that there is no abruptness in the flow of ideas and the smoothness of expression.

Clauses: A group of words containing a subject and predicate and functioning as a part of a compound or complex sentences. A semicolon is used to separate independent clauses without a coordinating convention.

Comma fault: The use of a comma instead of a semicolon to link two independent clauses. This is a major syntax error. It is sometimes called a comma splice.

Compound sentences: Two or more independent clauses joined by a coordinating conjunction, or a semicolon.

Economy of expression: Say only what needs to be said. Avoid noun strings. Eliminate redundancy, overuse of the passive voice, and detailed descriptions. Do not use clumsy prose. Do not elaborate or embellish. Short words and short sentences are easier to understand than are long ones.

Jargon: Jargon is the continuous use of technical vocabulary even in places where it is relevant. Jargon is also the substituting of a euphemistic phrase for a familiar term. *Momentarily felt scarcity* for *poverty*, and you should scrupulously avoid such jargon.

Orderly presentation of ideas: Thought units must be presented in an orderly manner. In this way readers will understand what you are presenting. To do this you must aim for continuity in words, concepts, and thematic development throughout your paper. Continuity can be achieved through punctuation. They cue the reader to pauses, inflections, subordination, and pacing normally heard in speaking.

Precision and clarity: Say only what is needed. If you are frugal with words you will write a more readable manuscript. You can tighten long papers by eliminating redundancy, wordiness, jargon, evasiveness, overuse of passive voice, and clumsy prose. Eliminate overly detailed descriptions, gratuitous embellishments, elaboration of the obvious, and irrelevant observations or asides.

Redundancy: Writers can become redundant in an effort to be emphatic. Use no more words than are necessary to convey meaning. Do not embellish or repeat for emphasis.

Run on sentences: Compound sentences in which independent clauses are not separated by punctuation or a connecting conjunction. This is a major syntax error.

Sentence fragment: A group of words that is not a complete sentence, but is punctuated as one. *If it mattered greatly.* This is a major syntax error.

Sentence length: While most of your writing will be in short simple sentences, you must avoid abruptness or choppiness. Varied sentence length helps maintain interest and comprehension. Direct, declarative sentences with simple common words are usually best.

Simple sentence: A short direct, declarative sentence with a subject-verb or a subject-verb-objective configuration. Use clear, concise, and cogent simple sentences throughout most of your paper.

Wordiness: Unconstrained wordiness lapses into embellishment and flowery writing and are inappropriate in formal writing. Wordiness can impede the ready grasp of ideas.

Other Grammar Issues

Adjective: A word or words that describe a noun.

Adverb: A word or words that modifies a verb, adjective, adverb preposition phrase, clause, or sentence.

Agreement: A grammatical relationship that involves the correspondence in number either between subject and verb in a sentence or between a pronoun and its antecedent.

Case: The form of a noun or pronoun that reflects it grammatical function in a sentence as subject (they), object (them), or possessor (their). For example: *She* gave *her* employees a raise that pleased *them* greatly.

Colloquialism: A word or expression appropriate to informal conversation but not usually suitable for formal writing. Colloquialisms diffuse meaning.

Comparisons: Ambiguous or illogical comparison result from omission of key verbs or from nonparallel structure. An illogical comparison occurs when parallelism is overlooked for the sake of brevity. *Her salary was lower than a convenience store clerk* instead of *Her salary was lower than that of a convenience store clerk.*

He/she Avoid the overuse of he/she when referring to one person where gender is not known. In most cases the sentence can be rewritten to avoid the he/she.

Noun: A word that names a person, place, thing or idea.

Preposition: A word that relates its object to another word in the sentence.

Pronoun: Any of a small group of words that are used for substitutes for nouns, phrases, or clauses and refer to someone or something named or understood in context.

Proper noun: The name of a particular person, place, or thing. Proper nouns are capitalized. Common nouns name classes of people, places, and things and are not capitalized.

Tense: The time of a verb's action or state of being, such as past, present, or future. *Saw, see, will see.* In formal writing past tense and present perfect tenses (has been) are used throughout the paper except in the interpretation part of the discussion section. Conclusions and recommendations can be written in past tense, present tense, or in future tense. Tense errors are very common in formal writing and should be carefully avoided.

Unbiased language: When referring to a person or persons choose words that are accurate, clear, and free from bias. For example using *man* to refer to all human beings is not as acceptable the phrase *men and women. Gender* is the term to use when referring to men and women as social groups. Writing without bias is recognizing that differences should be mentioned only when relevant.

Verb: a word or group of words that expresses the action or indicates the state of being of the subject. Verbs activate sentences.

Writing Tips

It is important that you follow these grammatical expectations in terms of punctuation, syntax, and other issues of grammar. Whenever you have concerns about the structure of sentences, the correct or appropriate punctuation to use, how to ensure the orderly flow of information, and to ensure economy of expression you should refer to this section of the *Handbook* and to the writing tips following each of the sections of the *Handbook*. It is your obligation as a writer of formal papers to learn these grammatical expectations and to use them effectively in your paper. We have suggested other sources that are more complete and suggest that you use at least one for additional grammar specifics and information.

In this glossary of terms are entries, many of which you will use in your review of literature or in your research study. Others are included that you may need as you review literature and other studies related to your paper or research study.

A

Action research. Research done by a practitioner in single case studies or small group interventions.

Analysis of covariance (ANCOVA). A procedure for determining whether the difference between the mean scores of two or more groups on one or more dependent variables is statistically significant.

Analytic induction. In qualitative research, the process of inferring themes and patterns from an examination of data.

Analytic reporting. In a qualitative research report, the use of an objective writing style where the researchers voice is silent or subdued and other conventions typical to quantitative research.

Anecdotal record. A record of behaviors or activities that occur at designated times or when the behaviors or activities occur.

Aptitude test. A measure of abilities that are assumed to be relevant to performance on an identified type of skill or area of achievement.

Artifacts. Objects created by members of past or present cultures.

Axiology. The study of the nature, types, and criteria of values, and value judgments especially in ethics.

B

Baseline. In single case studies the natural behavior patterns of the subject of the study.

Bias. Personal and unreasonable distortion of judgment in such a way that certain facts are habitually overlooked, distorted, or falsified.

C

Case study research. Study of a phenomenon in its natural context from the perspective of the participants.

Category. In the review of literature a major component of the review. There must be at least two in the review of literature. A component of frequency count data.

Chain of evidence. In qualitative research the validation of the study's findings by clear meaningful links in terms of the study's questions, the raw data analysis and findings.

Chi square. An inferential test of statistical significance used when research data are in the form of frequency counts in two or more categories.

Citation. Information about a document or resource that one would need in order to locate it. A citation contains the name of the author and the year of publication. It is in parantheses following the quotation or paraphrase. If no author is listed use the first two words of the title.

Cognitive taxonomy. A classification of cognition developed by Bloom and colleagues. Initially the taxonomy had six categories. This was revised to seven including: Memory, translation, interpretation, application, analysis, synthesis, and evaluation.

Cohort longitudinal research. An investigation in which changes in a population over time are studied by selecting a different sample at each data collection point from a population that remains constant.

Correlational research. An investigation that seeks to discover the direction and magnitude of the relationships between two or more variables through the use of correlational statistics.

Curriculum. What is to be taught to prepare students for a given purpose. Curriculum has structure and sequence. It contains content areas that are interrelated and interdependent.

D

Dependent variable. The variable the researcher is interested in measuring to determine how it is different for groups with different experience or characteristics.

Descriptor. A term or used to classify information about the topic in the classification of documents or to describe briefly categories of information.

Descriptive statistics. Statistical analyses which describe the data collected. They include mean, median, mode, range, and standard deviation. In qualitative research, investigation that involves providing a detailed portrayal of one or more cases.

Diagnostic test. A test used to determine a student's strengths and weaknesses in a particular subject.

Disaggregated data. Data reported in the results section on identified groups within the population tested.

E

Educational Resources Information Center (ERIC). A federally funded agency that provides information resources to the education community.

Emergent design. In qualitative studies, the practice of changing the design of the study or evaluation as the evaluator or researcher gains new insights into the concerns and issues of the group being studied.

Emic perspective. Research participants perceptions of their social reality.

Epistemology. The study of the nature of knowledge.

Experiential taxonomy. A *gestalt* taxonomy developed by Steinaker & Bell that incorporates the cognitive and affective taxonomies in a five step sequence that can be used for teaching and evaluating student work.

Ethnography. The in depth study of life in an identified culture and patterns within it. The focus is on society and culture. Ethnographic studies uncover and describe beliefs, values, and attitudes of a group.

Etic perspective. The researcher's perspective of the research participants social reality.

Experimenter bias. A situation in which the experimenter or author's expectations about what will occur are transmitted to the research participants behavior in the study is affected. Also a situation in which the researcher's expectations affect data collection and data analysis.

Extinction. The practice of behavior modification through the withdrawal of an intervention in behavioral research.

F

Formative evaluation. Evaluation of the process of a study done while the program is underway.

G

Generalizability. Researcher's ability to generalize results from the sample from which it was drawn and relate those generalizations to transferability.

Grounded theory. An approach to theory development in qualitative research. Grounded theory emerges from the data collected and the narrative associated with those data. It is an emergent theory and does not depend on an existing theory.

H

Hermeneutics. A field of inquiry that seeks to understand how individuals develop interpretations and consensus about issues and tasks.

Historical research. A study of past phenomena for the purpose of gaining a better understanding of present institutions, practices, trends, and issues.

Hypothesis. A researcher's prediction, derived from theory or from speculation, about how two or more variables will be related to each other.

I

Independent variable. The treatment or intervention the researcher uses with the experimental group in an experimental design within quantitative research.

Inferential statistics. Statistical protocols designed to determine significance.

Institutional review board (IRB). A committee established by an institution to ensure that participants in research projects will be protected from harm. The IRB reviews and approves research done by members of the institution.

Interrater reliability. A measure to determine if two or more raters reliably measure criteria with similar standards and results.

Interval recording. The recording of observational behaviors at given time intervals.

Item analysis. A set of procedures for determining the difficulty, the reliability, and the validity of each item on a test.

Iteration. A repeated procedure intended to bring to participants in a study or students to a predetermined level of competence

L

Likert scale. A measure that asks individuals to check their level of agreement with various statements.

Longitudinal research. An investigation that involves describing changes in a sample's characteristics over a specified period of time.

M

Matrix. In a qualitative research report, a type of table that has defined rows and columns for reporting the results of data analyses and other information.

Mean. A measure of central tendency calculated by the sum of the score in a set by the numbers of scores.

Median. A measure of central tendency corresponding to the middle score in a range of scores.

Meta analysis. Statistical procedures to identify trends from the results of a set of studies on the same problem or issue.

Mode. A measure of central tendency corresponding to the most frequently occurring score in a distribution of scores.

Monograph. A professional treatise on a narrow area of learning.

Multiple regression. A statistical procedure for determining the relationship between a criterion variable and a combination of two or more predictor variables.

N

NCE score. A type of scoring with a mean of 50. The scores are continuous and have an equality of units. There are 100 scores in all and they correspond to individual percentages.

Normal curve. A distribution of scores that form a symmetrical, bell shaped curve when plotted on a graph.

O

Objectivity. The extent to which the narrative or the scores on a test by the biases of the researcher or the writer.

Ontology. A branch of metaphysics concerned with the nature and relations of being, the kinds of existents or having being.

Ordinal scale. A measure in which numbers represent a rank ordering of individuals or objects on some variable.

Outlier. A research participant's score on a measure which differs markedly from other scores.

P

Parameter. The boundary of a study, a series of scores, or the characteristics of a population's scores.

Paraphragiarism. Borrowing of another author's writing to such an extent as to constitute the representation of the other author's work as your own. Similar to plagiarism.

Pattern. In qualitative research instances in which certain behaviors, attitudes, or actions are systematically related to each other.

Pearson r. In correlational statistical analysis a mathematical expression of the direction and magnitude of the relationship between two measures with continuous scores.

Percentile. A type of rank score that represents a raw score as the percentage of individuals in the norming group whose scores fall below that score.

Personal communication. An interview with a peer or other person which is cited or quoted in the text of a paper.

Pilot study. A small scale preliminary investigation conducted to develop and test the measures used in a research study.

Positivism. An epistemological belief that reality is independent of those who observe it, and that observations of this reality, if unbiased, constitute scientific knowledge.

Postmodernism. A broad social and philosophical movement that questions the rationality of human action, the use of positivist epistemology, and any human endeavor that claims a privileged position with respect to the search for truth.

Posttest. A measure that is administered following an experimental or control treatment in order to determine the effects of the intervention. A posttest only is a test given to both experimental and control groups following the intervention with the experimental group.

Presentism. Interpreting past events in terms of concepts and perspectives that originated in recent times.

Pretest. A measure administered prior to an experimental treatment or other intervention.

Q

Qualitative research. Inquiry that is grounded in the assumption that individuals construct social reality in the form of meaning and interpretations, and that these constructions tend to be transitory and situational.

Quantitative research. Inquiry that is grounded in the assumption that features of the social environment constitute and objective reality that is relatively constant across time and settings.

R

Random assignment. The process of assigning individuals or groups to the experimental or control treatment in order that each individual or group has an equal chance of being in each group.

Range. The difference between the highest and the lowest scores in a distribution.

Reliability. The extent to which a test yields the same or similar results in repeated administration.

Rubric. A scale to measure different levels of proficiency demonstrated by students.

S

Sampling. The process of selecting members of a research sample from a defined population.

Semantic differential scale. A measure that asks individuals to rate an attitude on a series of bipolar adjective (fair-unfair, valuable-worthless, hot-cold).

Semiotics. The study of sign systems. In particular the study of how objects come to meaning and how sign systems affect human behavior.

Snowball sampling. Cases that are selected by asking one person to recommend others with similar experiences.

Stakeholder. Participants in a study who have an interest in the quality and outcomes of a program. Can be program employees, parents, citizens, or students.

Standard deviation. A measure of the extent that scores in a distribution deviate from their mean.

Statistic. Any number that describes a characteristic of a sample's score on a measure.

Survey research. The use of questionnaires or interviews to collect data about the characteristics, experiences, knowledge, or, opinions of a sample or a population.

T

t **Score.** A probability distribution used to determine level of statistical significance of an obtained *t* value of the difference between two sample means.

Test. A structured performance situation that can be analyzed to yield numerical scores.

Theory. An explanation of the commonalities and the relationships among observed phenomena in terms of casual structure and processes that are presumed to underlie them.

Triangulation. The use of multiple data collection methods, data sources, analysts, or theories a corroborative evidence for the validity of qualitative research findings.

V

Validity. Measures which determine if the test or measure for data collection is consistent with the content of what is being tested.

Variable. A characteristic of the sample of the population. Data from the characteristic are collected, analyzed and reported.

This paper is designed to provide you with a model of what your formal paper should look like. It is a review of literature paper, not a research paper. In a research paper you would include the method section and the results section. Most of what we have presented earlier about formal papers has been included in this review of literature. You have the model of the title page and the abstract. Elements of the introduction follow the material we have presented earlier in the book. You can see how the review of literature has been organized. The introductory paragraph, the categories and subcategories follow the format we have suggested. You can read and see how to do your discussion section including summary, interpretation, conclusions, and recommendations.

There are many models for references. You can use the reference included in this paper as well as the model references in Appendix E to learn how to prepare references for your own paper. As you prepare your own formal paper you can use this paper to identify format, sequence, categories, and subcategories. Note the sentence structure and the flow of ideas in the paper. Understanding syntax, structure, and sequence of the paper can be valuable to you as you write your own paper. Use this paper along with the materials in the body of this work to help you prepare the best possible formal paper you can. Please note that the page numbers are not sequential with the book, rather, they follow the page sequence of the model paper.

Standards and   1

Running head: STANDARDS AND PLANNING

Standards and Creative Planning

Norman W. Terry

National University

Standards and   2

Abstract

The purpose of this paper was to review literature on standards, creative planning, and teaching. The use of standards implied performance based instruction with demonstrated outcomes. It was shown that how one teaches was more important to learning than what was taught. Standards have been written to define what was to be taught. They have also been open for utilization of creative methodology. Teachers who planned carefully and used standards to create learning experiences could provide interactive learning at high cognitive levels. It was concluded that creative teaching augmented student learning. It was also concluded that all lessons must reach at least the application level of cognition. It was recommended that teachers receive professional development on creative implementation of standards.

Standards and Creative Planning

The purpose of this paper was to review literature about standards and how planning standards-based instruction could be related to creative and effective teaching. Standards, for the purpose of this paper, were defined as state standards used by states as the expectations for student achievement and demonstrated performance (California State, n. d.).

This topic has been a major area of focus for educators in all states. Darling-Hammond (2001) noted that standards "have become a major policy vehicle" (p.211). It was further noted that state standards should "be designed as a shell within which the kernel of professional judgment and decision making can function comfortably "(Shulman, 1983, p. 501). Learning should, with careful planning, be an experience the student can internalize (Steinaker & Bell, 1979). Reeves (2002) observed that every lesson and daily activity should relate to an identified standard. In order to implement a standards driven instructional program, teachers should "identify the best practices in standards-based teaching and learning" (Reeves, 2002, p. 53). Every lesson or activity should achieve at least the application level of cognition. A linked series of lessons should develop student learning at the analysis, synthesis, and evaluation levels of cognition (Steinaker, 2006b).

When teachers have planned lessons based on standards, the "how of teaching becomes more important than what we teach" (Steinaker, 2007b, p. 4). This meant that teachers must focus on experiential learning and helping students internalize what they have been exposed to, participated with, identified as important, and internalized. Furthermore, they needed to be able to disseminate what they have learned (Steinaker & Bell, 1979). Standards, in this context have become performance goals, that allowed the teacher to plan carefully and to include creativity as a major dimension of instruction. Thus, the teacher and the student could work together creatively and interactively to achieve the performance standard. Creativity became a sequential and integral part of the context of learning and provided the students with the ability to demonstrate the performance implicit within the standard (Steinaker, 2006b). Steinaker (2007b) further stated that the use of standards provided a basis and incentive for creative and experiential learning. It was concluded by Reeves (2002) that "teachers who create effective standards-based performance assignments are the real heroes of the standards movement" (p. 140).

I chose this topic because I wanted to investigate standards-based education as it related to creative planning and to the instructional process. I have believed that the more informed I became about implementing a creative instructional program, the more effective I could become as a teacher.

Review of Literature

This review of literature was organized with three categories. They were state standards, lesson planning with standards, and creativity and standards. The category on lesson planning had two subcategories. They were standards-based planning and heuristic electronic lesson planner.

State Standards

Every state has developed standards or performance descriptors (Reeves, 2002). Each state has its unique structure and organization. Some states provide standards and performance outcomes and little else. Other states detail support materials, references, suggested teaching strategies and examples (Education World, 2006). Each state has developed a specific format for its standards or performance outcomes. Teachers in Idaho, for example, were provided with grade level standards K-12 in all content areas along with identified goals and objectives for each grade level. They further provide standard assessments by grade level, information on professional development, and curriculum materials (Education World, 2006). Iowa was the only state not having standards. Instead they have performance level descriptors (Education World, 2006). Each state department of education provided some support information for teachers to help them in working with students for achieving the standards (Education World, 2006). In almost every state there were many standards in all content areas and at all grade

levels (Education World, 2006). Darling-Hammond (2002) saw standards

as a means to reform or transform schools. She conceptualized standards

as a means of transforming teaching and involving students in the process

of learning. She expressed concern about the number of standards and the

expectation that the teachers need to cover each standard. She further felt

there needed to be fewer standards and more in depth learning (Darling-

Hammond, 2002). Shulman (1983) described standards as being

"designed as a shell within which the kernel of professional judgment and

decision making can function comfortably" (p. 501).

The use of standards or generic objectives has not been a new

phenomenon in American education. Franklin Bobbitt, in 1924, organized

a course of study for the elementary grades.

> He outlined more than 800 objectives and related activities to coincide
>
> with predetermined student needs. These activities ranges from 'the
>
> ability to care for [one's] teeth . . . eyes . . . nose . . . and throat; . . . to
>
> keep home appliances in good working condition; . . . spelling and
>
> grammar.' Bobbitt's methods were quite sophisticated for his day
>
> (Ornstein & Hunkins, 2004, p. 3).

The issue of standards has been a part of the American educational

scene since the late seventies. Debates have been continuing. "As the world becomes increasingly complex, standards appropriate in simpler times are no longer adequate. In an information age, students [must] meet higher demands on their levels of knowledge and skills than did their counterparts in a pre industrial nation" (Ornstein & Hunkins, 2004, p. 393).

Based on this premise states have responded with the development of standards for teachers to use as performance evidence for student achievement (Steinaker, 2006b). Models of teaching could be related to standards. Joyce, Weil, and Calhoun (2004) linked each model of teaching they identified with student achievement and student performance.

There have been issues in state support for standards-based instruction. A critical issue according to authors at the North Central Regional Educational Laboratory, was resources to support higher student achievement. They indicated that

> creating standard-based schools that are accountable for helping all students reach higher levels of achievement requires schools and districts to rethink their educational resources—especially time, staffing, and money. As districts begin to support schools in becoming increasingly accountable for results, they are finding that schools need: more time for students in academic subjects and more individualized attention; time and dollars for ongoing teacher professional development and planning; and investment funding for the purchase, introduction, and classroom implementation of new curriculum

materials and teaching practices aimed at higher standards (North

Central, 2006, p. 1)

This was but one issues. There have been many other issues. For

example, how to teach to standards has been another. In this area, state

departments of education have provided differentiated kinds of support

(Education World, 2006). Steinaker (2007b) suggested that professional

development be provided for teachers to creatively plan how to teach to

the standards in an interactive and creative environment. State personnel

have defined performance standards (Education World, 2006). Corollary

to student achievement of the performance expected within the standard

was the need for "more autonomy and authority in the use of time, the

selection and use of staff, and the alignment of funds (North Central, 2006

p. 1) Further, it has been confirmed that if students had more time focused

on academics they could learn more (Prisoners of, 1994). There were other

issues and there have been personnel in all states addressing them

(Education World, 2006).

Lesson Planning With Standards

Critical to successful student learning has been careful and creative

planning. Steinaker and Harrison (1976) noted that "a carefully structured

instructional program contribute[s] to student [learning]. . . . The

importance of a structured curriculum and instructional program emerges as the most important factor, in determining whether a student does achieve as expected (pp. 75–76).

Standards based planning. Lesson planning focused on achieving performance based standards is essential (Steinaker, 2006b). There are many theoretical perspectives on how students learn (Ornstein & Hunkins, 2004). Bruner (1961) felt that learning involved organizing meaningful experiences which could be transferred more readily than rote learning. Dewey (1910) identified this dimension of learning as reflective thinking. In a standards-based instructional environment, there has been a need for teachers to carefully plan and sequence a variety of teaching strategies for all students to learn experientially and interactively (Steinaker & Bell, 1979). Serdyukov (2004) indicated that "lesson planning is essential in . . . any aspect of daily classroom life" (p. 5). Furthermore, "it has become important that the relationship between the skills and concepts to be learned be clearly related to and drawn from specific standards. The achievement standards needed to be kept personal and cooperative, not competitive." (Steinaker & Leavitt, 2007). Reeves (2004) stated that "academic standards make it clear that students cannot be complacent about 'beating' a competitor; they must persist, work, and learn until they meet the standard" (p. 27). Planning should be based on the achievement of standards. This is the imperative of the state education standards and performance level descriptors (Education World, 2006).

Heuristic electronic lesson planner. One program for teaching planning keyed to the standards and other professional expectations was the *Heuristic Electronic Lesson Planner* (HELP) developed by Steinaker (2007a). Teachers who have used the program log in, identify the state for which they wanted standards, selected the grade level, and the content area. When this was completed the standards for that content area and grade level were shown on the screen and the teacher selected the standard on which the students were to work. The teacher then entered the lesson objective in the space provided. Time and date of the lesson were determined by the teacher. Teachers could, on a pop up menu, choose the primary classroom structure used and the technology pertinent to the lesson. These were on pop up menus (Steinaker, 2007a). From a list of twenty-five sequenced teaching strategies, the teacher chose the ones to be used. These strategies were keyed to the cognitive taxonomy and when the strategy deepest into the list of strategies was chosen, the level of cognition for that lesson was shown in the space for cognition on the program. Likewise the teacher chose strategies for specially designed activities in English (SDAIE). In addition, the teacher selected assessment strategies from a pop up menu. Finally in a space provided, the teacher wrote each of the sequential steps in the lesson. After the lesson was completed, in the same space, the teacher could write the results of the lesson. The lesson could then be printed. In this way the teacher had a running record of each

Standards and   11

standard taught, of each teaching strategy and SDAIE strategy used, the

sequence of the lesson, and the outcome of the lesson (Steinaker, 2007a).

In addition to the format described above, there was documentation

and information about each of the categories noted (Steinaker, 2007a)

This was available to the teacher by clicking on a help button linked to the

category. Information about that category was immediately available to

the teacher. Professional support for the teacher was provided about the

cognitive taxonomy, teaching strategies, classroom structures, SDAIE

strategies, types of group structures, assessments, technologies, and

classroom instructional organizations (Steinaker, 2007a). This was the only

known program that had professional documentation built into it.

Teachers who have used the program like it. One said that the program was

"really terrific" (Personal communication B. Holzner, November 9, 2006).

Building lessons around standards has become for them a natural and

effective and creative planning modality (Steinaker, 2006). As Serdyukov

(2004) indicated, "effective lesson planning helps you stay focused"

(p. 20). Effective lesson planning through HELP provided a professional

and creative format for lesson planning (Steinaker, 2007a).

Creativity and Standards

The how of teaching, as noted by Steinaker (2006b) was more

important than the what of teaching. State standards identify the what of teaching (Educational World, 2006). The how of teaching is directly related to creativity. Steinaker and Bell (1979) defined creativity as having five levels. They were "motivation to develop a product, visualization of the product, experimenting with ways to complete the product, actually completing the product, and finally admiring it, showing it, and sharing it" (p. 90). They further identified creativity as "a personal interaction with an idea, with material, or a problem. It is a process that requires sequences and activity unique to the individual and that results in a product, and acquires skill, or a modified behavior" (p. 91).

This definition of creativity along with HELP (Steinaker, 2007a) has provided for teachers a methodology for creating interactive learning experiences for students. Brown and Palinscar, 1989) defined this kind of interactive learning and reciprocal teaching. Joyce, Weil, and Calhoun (2004) defined reciprocal teaching as intrinsic to scaffolding which could help students "acquire increasing metacognitive control" (p. 15). As teachers involved in creative and reciprocal learning experiences, "they know how to take the initiative in planning . . . and they know how to work with others. . . . These students are both challenging and exhilarating to teach" (Joyce et al., 2004, p. 9). Teachers must learn to teach experientially and trust students to become involved with these kinds of interactive learning (Steinaker, 2007b). In order to ensure that motivation and creativity occurred in planing, teachers must not only trust students

Standards and   13

but must "authentically commit themselves [and] examine themselves constantly" (Freire, 2006, p. 60). "Professional teaching is a process of giving and receiving, of sharing and listening, and of visioning and achieving. Creativity and challenge are the underpinnings of these dimensions of professional teaching" (Steinaker, 2006b, p. 2). Reeves has noted that "teachers who create effective standards-based performance assignments are the heroes of education" (p. 140). Every teacher has become a leader and every student has shared in that leadership. "Leadership is a passionate exercise toward the implementation of a personal and a shared vision" (Steinaker, 2005 p. 1). "Synectics [creativity] is used to help us develop fresh ways of thinking about the student, the student's motives, the nature of penalties, our goals, and the nature of the problem" (Joyce et al., 2004, p. 163). Standards based planning has been an essential incentive toward creativity and interactive teaching (Steinaker, 2006a). This perspective was best stated by a student who said

> education is not a destination, but is a journey that continues in the hearts and minds of teachers who love and care for their students. May we all begin that journey with continuity, commitment, courage, community, and compassion. May we engage students in dialogue and direction so that they may find purpose and continue their personal journey positively and with integrity. (Steinaker, 2006a p. 3.)

Discussion

Summary

Standards have "become a major policy vehicle" (Darling-Hammond 2001, p. 211) Personnel in every state have developed standards or performance descriptors (Reeves, 2002). Darling-Hammond (2001) saw the use of standards as a means of reform or transformation of the schools. She also suggested that there should be fewer standards and more in depth learning. It was noted that learning should be an experience which students could internalize (Steinaker & Bell, 1979). When teachers planned lessons the "how of teaching becomes more important than what we teach" (Steinaker, 2006b, p. 2). Standards are not new to American education. As early as 1924 Bobbitt suggested more than 800 goals for students. Ornstein and Hunkins (2004) noted that students in an information age must "meet higher demands on their levels of knowledge and skills" (p. 393). This required a "carefully structured curriculum and instructional program" (Steinaker & Harrison, 1976, pp. 75–76). Bruner (1959) felt that learning involved organized experiences which could be transferred. Dewey (1910) called this reflective thinking. Serdyukov (2004) called lesson planning "essential" (p. 5). A major problem in performance based instruction has been resources (North Central, 2006). HELP has been one such resource. It was a lesson planning format which was professional in structure and purpose and which allowed for creativity and in depth learning (Steinaker 2006b). Within this program, using links to professional documentation, support was immediately available to teachers. Steinaker & Bell, 1979) defined creativity as having five sequential steps. They suggested that teachers use creative learning experiences which involve students in planning. Further it was noted that motivation and creativity occur in planning when teachers "authentically commit themselves" to teaching (Freire, 2006, p. 60). Joyce et al., 2004) called these involved students "challenging and exhilarating to teach" (p. 9). Steinaker (2007b) noted this as interactive learning. Finally it was suggested by Steinaker (2006b) that standards-based planning was an incentive toward creativity and interactive teaching.

Interpretation

Standards are not new to American education. I agree with Ornstein & Hunkins (2004) that they have been with us from the twenties. Since all states have standards or performance descriptors (Reeves, 2002), I believe, with Serdyukov (2004) that careful planning and instruction are essential to student learning. I further believe that the effective use of standards can reform or even bring about transformation in schools (Darling-Hammond, 2002). I also concur with authors at North Central Regional Educational

Laboratory (2006) that one of the major issues in standards-based
instructional programs is resources. Central to this issue is that teachers
and schools are "becoming increasingly accountable for results (p.1).
Steinaker and Harrison (1976) posited that careful planning is the most
important factor in student achievement. I concur with this view. HELP
(Steinaker, 2007a) is one such resource for teachers in terms of creative
lesson planning. I believe that this program can become a professional
resource for teachers and schools. I also agree with Joyce et al., 2004)
that teachers can link each model of teaching to student performance
and student achievement of performance based standards. Reflective
teaching (Dewey, 1910), transfer learning (Bruner, 1961) and reciprocal
teaching (Brown & Palinscar, 1989) are also ways of defining interactive
teaching, learning, and evaluation. I agree with Steinaker and Bell
(1979) that creativity can be defined and has five observable steps. This
creative teaching requires commitment on the part of teachers (Freire,
2006) and creative planning and instruction to "develop fresh ways of
thinking (Joyce et al., 2004). Finally, I agree with Steinaker (2006a) that
standards-based planning, instruction, and evaluation are strong
incentives toward creativity and interactive teaching and that "education
is not a destination, but is a journey that continues in the hearts and
minds of teachers who love and care for their students" (Steinaker,
2006a).

Standards and   17

Conclusions and Recommendations

Based on the review of literature and on my interpretation of the literature reviewed, I have concluded that the effective use of standards-based planning and instruction can result in creative teaching and augmented student learning. I have also concluded that there are programs such as HELP which can become an incentive to creative planning and teaching. Finally, I have concluded that in every lesson students must reach at least the application level of cognition.

Based on the review of literature, my interpretation, and conclusions, I recommend that teachers receive professional development on creative planning and implementation of standards. I further recommend that teachers use programs such as HELP as the format for their planning.

References

Brown, A. & Palinscar, A. (1989). Guided cooperative learning, individual knowledge acquisition. In L. Resnick (Ed.). *Knowing, learning, and instruction* (pp. 393–451. Hillsdale, NJ: Erlbaum.

Bruner, J. (1961). *The process of education.* Cambridge, MA: Harvard University Press.

California State Department of Education. (n.d.). *Content standards.* Retrieved November 21, 2006 from http://www.cde.ca.gov./be/st/ss-12k

Darling-Hammond, L. (2002). *The right to learn: A blueprint for creating schools that work.* San Francisco, CA: Jossey-Bass.

Dewey, J. (1910). *How we think.* Boston,: Heath.

Education World. (2006). National and state standards. Retrieved November 21 from http://www.education-world.com/standards/state/index.shtml

Freire, P. (2006). *Pedagogy of the oppressed.* New York: The Continuum International Publishing Group, Inc.

Joyce, B., Weil, M., & Calhoun, E. (2004) *Models of teaching* (7th ed.) Boston: Pearson Education, Inc.

North Central Regional Educational Laboratory (2006). Critical issue: Rethinking the use of educational resources to support higher student achievement. Retrieved November 24, 2006 from http://www.ncrel.org/sdrs/areas/issues/envirnmnt/go/go600.htm

Standards and   19

Ornstein, A. C. & Hunkins, F. P. (2004) *Curriculum foundations, principles, and issues.* (4th ed.) Boston: Pearson Education, Inc.

Prisoners of time: The report of the national education commission on time and learning. (1994) Washington, DC: United States Printing Office.

Reeves, D. B. (2002). *Making standards work: How to implement standards-based assessment in the classroom, school, and district.* Denver, CO: Advanced Learning Press.

Serdyukov, P. (2004) *Effective lesson planning.* Boston: Pearson Custom Publishers.

Shulman, L. (1983). Autonomy and obligation. In L. Shulman & G. Sykes (Eds.), *Handbook of teaching and policy* (pp. 484–504). White Plains, NY: Longman.

Steinaker, N. W. (2005). *Leadership.* Unpublished manuscript, National University.

Steinaker, N. W. (2006a) *Critical pedagogy: A perspective.* Unpublished manuscript, National University.

Steinaker, N. W. (2006b). *Using standards for professional planning.* Unpublished manuscript, National University.

Steinaker, N. W. (2007a) *Heuristic electronic lesson planner.* Trabuco Canyon, CA: Communications L.T.D.

Steinaker, N. W. (2007b). Standards as incentives for creativity. Trabuco Canyon, CA: Communications L.T.D.

Steinaker, N. W. & Bell, M. R. (1979) *The experiential taxonomy: A new approach to teaching and learning.* New York: Academic Press.

Steinaker, N. W. & Harrison, M. (1976). *Measuring experiences through the experiential taxonomy.* Ontario, CA: Ontario-Montclair School District.

Steinaker, N. W. & Leavitt, L. S. (2007). *Simulation: An adventure in learning.* Trabuco Canyon, CA: Communications L.T.D.